A New Politics
from the Left

Radical Futures
Hilary Wainwright, *A New Politics from the Left*

Hilary Wainwright

———

A New Politics from the Left

polity

First published in 2018 by Polity Press

Polity Press
65 Bridge Street
Cambridge CB2 1UR, UK

Polity Press
101 Station Landing
Suite 300
Medford, MA 02155, USA

ISBN-13: 978-1-5095-2362-7
ISBN-13: 978-1-5095-2363-4 (pb)

A catalogue record for this book is available from the British Library.

Library of Congress Cataloging-in-Publication Data
Names: Wainwright, Hilary, author.
Title: A new politics from the left / Hilary Wainwright.
Description: Cambridge, UK ; Medford, MA, USA : Polity Press, 2018. | Series:
    Radical futures | Includes bibliographical references and index.
Identifiers: LCCN 2017040345 (print) | LCCN 2017059039 (ebook) | ISBN
    9781509523665 (Epub) | ISBN 9781509523627 (hardback) | ISBN 9781509523634
    (pb)
Subjects: LCSH: Liberalism. | Democracy. | Right and left (Political science)
Classification: LCC JC574 (ebook) | LCC JC574 .W34 2018 (print) | DDC
    320.53--dc23
LC record available at https://lccn.loc.gov/2017040345

Typeset in 11 on 15 Sabon by Servis Filmsetting Ltd, Stockport, Cheshire
Printed and bound in the United Kingdom by Clays Ltd, St Ives PLC

For further information on Polity, visit our website: politybooks.com

To the memories of:

Andy Wainwright, whose intense and inquiring
personality I will never forget

Roy Bhaskar, whose wisdom and warmth
will always strengthen me

Doreen Massey, whose sharp wit and insight
influence my thoughts

Robin Murray, whose inspiring vision and
well-grounded optimism guide me always

Contents

Preface

Writing as I have in the middle and at the end of an election campaign, I found the advice of Italo Calvino useful: 'I reject the role of the person chasing events. I prefer the person who continues his discourse, waiting for it to become topical again, like all things that have a sound basis.'[1]

It's not for me but for the reader to judge whether my discourse has a sound basis. And I will not chase the events leading up to election day, or the extraordinary surge of support for Jeremy Corbyn against Theresa May, or the details of the repercussions for the Labour Party and Momentum. I hope, though, that my arguments will be a resource for the diverse movement that helped to produce this surge, as it experiments with ways to maintain its energy, creativity and stubborn determination to create an open, participatory, green and feminist form of socialism – leaving the question of whether the Labour Party can become the vehicle of such a socialism as one that I cannot answer with any certainty, but to which I would, if pressed, reply with a cautious and conditional 'yes'. Certainly, it is an objective worth working for, while remaining alert to the fact that such a change will face determined and vicious opposition.

A new politics from the left is in the making and its fully formed character cannot usefully be predicted at this point – or prescribed. Hence, I envisage this book as but one contribution to a widely collaborative and participatory political work in progress. It is not a manifesto for a new politics from the left but, rather, a limited contribution based on exploring one line of argument, concerning the fundamental importance of a new politics of knowledge – of whose knowledge matters, and what counts as knowledge anyway; and also exploring how understandings of knowledge underpin understandings of power, in practice as much as in theory. For it is in practice that innovations are first created.

Acknowledgements

The ideas of this book have been long in incubation. First, I must thank Fiona Dove and Daniel Chavez, at the Transnational Institute (TNI). Together we founded the TNI's New Politics Project, to work with social movements as they engaged with political parties and the state. I am very grateful for the support – financial, political and intellectual – of the TNI as a whole, over many years, and especially to Phyllis Bennis, the late Praful Bidwai, Brid Brennan, Nick Buxton, Susan George, Satoko Kishimoto, Edgardo Lander, Susan Medeiros, Achin Vanaik and Pietje Vervest.

A vital part of the incubation took place through the Networked Politics seminars that I organized with my dear *compañeros* Marco Berlinguer and Mayo Fuster Morell. Many of the ideas in this book were first expressed in these seminars and in later work together.

I also want to thank my co-editors and comrades at *Red Pepper* magazine, both on the editorial collective and on the board. They have been a rich source of inspiration and challenge, both in person and in the magazine itself, which I think readers of this book would also find an invaluable resource.

Next, I must thank my editor at Polity, George Owers, for commissioning the book and for being such an exemplary editor: encouraging, firm and ruthless at appropriate moments. Instead of being fazed by a manuscript 20,000 words over-length, he calmly improved the book by suggesting careful cuts, with the help of anonymous reviewers to whom I am also very grateful. Others helped to whip the sprawling manuscript into shape, most notably *Red Pepper*'s editorial alchemist Steve Platt; the TNI's doyenne of sub-editors, Deborah Eade; and finally, Polity's ever-patient, ever-intelligent copy-editor Leigh Mueller.

In the writing, I drew on a number of formal and informal interviews and collaborations with those who are creating and reporting on the emerging new politics. I only have space to list them; it will be clear in the text how much I owe to them: Christophe Aguiton, Michel Bauwens, Matt Brown,

Acknowledgements

Michael Calderbank, Andrew Dolan, Theano Fotiou, Ashish Ghadiali, Jeremy Gilbert, Christos Giovanopoulos, Mike Hales, Paul Hilder, Vedran Horvat, Ewa Jasiewicz, Andreas Karitzis, Adam Klug, Christos Korolis, Jon Lansman, Neal Lawson, Nick Mahoney, Robin McAlpine, John McDonnell MP, Ioannis Margaris, Alex Nunns, Ben Sellers, Jonathan Shafi, Joan Subirats, Euclid Tsakalotos, Tom Walker, and my friends and comrades in Hackney Momentum, especially Charlie Clarke, Liz Davies and Heather Mendick, who read and commented on early drafts. Finally, Margie Mendell, Cilla Ross and Stephen Yeo were immensely helpful on the many-sided experience of the co-operative movement. I must thank Ed Dingwall, too, who accurately transcribed the formal interviews.

I'd also like to mention my critically and radically minded nephews and nieces, Tom, Jessie, Olly, Annie and Rosie, who provided insights and challenges that kept me on my toes. My great-nieces, Emily, Olive and Frankie, and nephew Theo, have been a great diversion and source of hope for the future.

Writing requires concentration, and several people provided ideal places to focus single-mindedly, away from the hurly-burly of Hackney: the welcoming team at the Quaker retreat of Swarthmoor Hall; the redoubtable Jenny Hollis at Castaway

Acknowledgements

Cottages, Anglesey; Martin and Penny Wainwright with their library, intriguing conversation and necessary opportunities for exercise in Thrupp, Oxfordshire; Tessa Wainwright and Hugh Scott, who understood when I worked over most of their convivial Christmas; and Helen Winslow, who lent me her Saltaire bolthole in which to write in peace.

Finally, writing this book over the past year needed sustained morale, intellectual stimulus, challenge and occasional advice – as well as considerable patience – and for this I must thank my dear friends: Anthony Arblaster, Anthony Barnett, Huw Beynon, Sue Bowen, Luciana Castelina, Derek Clarke, Bob Colenutt, Anna Coote, Lawrence Cox, Evelina Dagnino, Barbara Epstein, Barbara Gunnell, Sue Himmelweit, Lioba Hirsch, Glenn Jenkins, Mary Kaldor, Marion Kozak, Richard Kuper, Maureen Mackintosh, Su Maddock, Bridget Maguire, Simon Mohun, Chantal Mouffe, Beth Murray, Frances Murray, William Outhwaite, Leo Panitch, Jenny Pearce, George Pope, Angie Raffle, Oscar Reyes, Mike Richardson, Sheila Rowbotham, Lynne Segal, Jane Shallice, Anne Slater, Sissy Vouvou, Mike Ward, Jo Warin and Pippa Warin.

All these people contributed to anything of merit in this book. I, however, take full responsibility for the whole.

1

A New Politics of Knowledge

The evident crisis of ruling political institutions across the world is also a crisis of how the ruling elites understand knowledge: whose and what kinds of knowledge they consider to be legitimate sources of expertise that matter for public policy. As with the widespread political crisis, this crisis of the politics of knowledge is a deep structural problem, not simply a character flaw of a particular elite.

These crises have historical roots. The events of 1968 and the immediate aftermath marked a turning point in the politics of knowledge: a leap in the desire for self-government. They signalled the breaking of the bond between knowledge and authority that underpinned the central post-war institutions: the paternalistic family and state, and the 'scientific' management that governed workplaces and the wider society. It was an understanding of knowledge that marginalized challenging insights and consequent debate arising from experience and practical expertise pointing beyond the dominant paradigm.[1]

Authority in all spheres of life and across the world was in question – and with it elite forms of knowledge. Rebel movements shared and developed their own kinds of knowledge, via practice and through debate and deliberations, and on to producing new ideas and the basis of new institutions. Authority, once it has been confidently questioned by those on whose obedience it depends, crumbles in ways that make it difficult to put together again.

In the UK, Margaret Thatcher used brutal methods to crush revolt – to starve striking miners and terrorize them into going back to work, and to axe local democracy in the towns and cities where the mining communities had allies. For several years, she was able to use the market and a foreign enemy (Argentina's military dictatorship) to renew a traditional acquiescence to authority, rooted in imperial and wartime success. But, in the end, she was brought down by revolt, in the streets and in her own cabinet.

Tony Blair also tried to re-establish the authority of ruling institutions. He sought to make the knowledge of those in authority unchallengeable, technical and apolitical and above the hoi polloi – a sacred sphere of technocratic expertise available only to those trained to know and beyond challenge from those whose expertise was not deemed sufficiently technocratic or 'professional'. While wooing 'swing' voters, he treated anyone connected to the public sector – or so-called 'losers' in the market casino – with contempt, as if their practical knowledge was irrelevant to the improvement of public services.

We have seen the elite contempt for the intelligence and know-how of Greek citizens in the recent behaviour of the European Union and its disregard for their democratic decisions. 'Elections cannot interfere with economics', declared German Finance Minister Wolfgang Schäuble when Greece's Finance Minister, Yanis Varoufakis, openly presumed that his government's mandate to reject the memorandum prescribed for the country by the Troika might have some influence on how the EU conducted its negotiations. This despite the fact that many Greek public servants were already willing to 'whistle-blow' in the public interest and share with the government their inside knowledge of the multiple sources of corruption.[2] Many such ethically minded public servants – teachers and doctors, for instance – were already working voluntarily to improve public services, albeit without the funds to do so, while Greek farmers, workers and social entrepreneurs were initiating alternative forms of production on a modest scale, with support from the Syriza government.

In the UK, we have seen contempt for everyday knowledge over Brexit – on both sides. The leading faction for Brexit had no shame in telling lies, making commitments, and then disappearing when it came to implementing them, as if voters were stupid. These anti-EU campaigners had no hesitation in playing on the racist imperial legacy among the white working class, bolstering assumptions of (white) British superiority. The government Remain side, as led by the then Prime Minister David Cameron, patronized voters with a visionless, simplistic campaign and, following its defeat, attacked Brexit voters as ignorant and stupid. As has since been established, there were many different reasons for the swathe of working-class support for Brexit, particularly in England and Wales, amounting to a rebellion expressing a sense of dispossession and deep class resentment, arising from the destruction of people's communities by successive governments – not stupidity at all.[3]

All these examples illustrate a politics of knowledge, because the questions that these and similar experiences raise about knowledge are entangled with the exercise of political power, especially at a time when official interpretations of politics are in question. Questions arose about whose knowledge – and whose future – matters in public policy, and what kinds of thoughts, ideas, beliefs, exchange of emotions and exercise of skills count as expertise and knowledge in public decision-making, and why. These are also questions about the basis on which our rulers rule: how they are accountable and how, when they behave in stupid, destructive or arrogant ways, they can be challenged.

Shock encounters with the free market in Central Europe

One particular experience shook me into taking the politics of knowledge seriously. The experience involved conversations with civic movement activists in Eastern Europe in 1990, following the fall of the Berlin Wall. It was the shock of witnessing the same young Czechs who had demonstrated in Wenceslas Square as part of the Velvet Revolution led by Václav Havel embracing Ronald Reagan and Margaret Thatcher as their heroes, and free-market theorist Friedrich von Hayek as their guru. As I wandered the streets of Prague, I was trying to puzzle out why impoverished students with no obvious vested interest in the free market would be so enamoured of its principles. How could those of us involved in social movements in the West sensitively challenge their illusion and convince them that socialism can be democratic?

First, it seemed to me, we had to understand the basis of their beliefs. So, after further discussions with Czech friends and an interview with Tomáš Ježek, Hayek's Czech translator (and Minister for Privatization at the time), I came to some preliminary conclusions.

The young Central and East Europeans were reacting to years of unremitting repression, based on the official justification that the state knew best what was good for them and for society. The assumption behind this command economy was that economic and social knowledge, narrowly understood as 'scientific' laws based on statistical correlations, could be centralized through the state. In his famous attack on state planning (by social democratic parties in the West as well as by the Kremlin) in *The Road to Serfdom* (1944), and his essay 'The Use of Knowledge in Society', Hayek had challenged the very nature of knowledge that this presumed.[4]

A New Politics of Knowledge

Tacit knowledge as the justification of the free market

Hayek argued that there is a type of knowledge, crucial to the economy and society, that by its very nature cannot be centralized. This is practical knowledge, the 'things we do but cannot tell', in the words of Michael Polanyi, who first theorized the idea of tacit knowledge. It is in the practitioner's head, but impossible to codify and thereby administer centrally.[5]

Hayek went further, arguing that such knowledge is necessarily *individual*. His exemplar was the intuitive knowledge of the individual entrepreneur. From here, it was a few short steps to justifying the price mechanism and the unregulated market as the only way that the individual practical, tacit knowledges of entrepreneurs and consumers could be co-ordinated.

Hayek celebrated as a mark of civilization what he called the 'haphazard' order that resulted from this unplanned, spontaneous co-ordination. Against the advocates of a planned economy, he insisted that those who planned, or who instructed the planners, could not possibly know the consequences of their plans and decisions, because of the individual, tacit character of this knowledge – limited, as he

7

assumed it is, to particular times and circumstances. In effect, he argued that we are socially blindfolded: such is the nature of economic and social knowledge. He concluded that any attempt to act as if this is not the case is positively dangerous, preparing the way for authoritarian government.

Answering the free-market right through the practical, social knowledge of social movements

It was understanding the appeal of this justification of the free market to young East Europeans, and straining to think how to answer it, that led me to recognize the importance of something right under my nose: in the social movements – the women's and radical shop stewards' movements, for example – in which I was active. There, in the practice of these movements, in the sharing of the practical and tacit knowledge that is the lifeblood of their organizations, was a crucial but under-theorized innovation.

They illustrated, in the way they organized, how this tacit knowledge might be shared – mutually and horizontally – and hence enable its holders to have knowledge beyond their own personal times and circumstances. Indeed, in their practice, these movements demonstrated the social production of knowledge, through reflection on experiences, the use of inherited theory and the application of intuition and tacit skill. (In fact, one of the main points made by Michael Polanyi, the principal theorist of tacit knowledge, was to highlight its importance in scientific experiments, which are essentially collaborative, social processes.)

Through this social process, such activists lift the blindfold. They come to understand – more or less, and subject to constant improvement – the consequences of their action. They do so through constantly reflecting on the lessons of experience. Hence, they are capable of purposeful and planned action, through collaboration and without predictive certainty, constantly subject to further experiment and self-reflexivity – a process that could be compared with the unpredictable yet purposeful character of modern jazz with its combination of structure and improvisation.

Tools to challenge Cold War dichotomies: 'the Berlin Wall did not fall on us'

This enables us, I concluded, to challenge the Cold War choice between the all-knowing state and the idea of the 'free market'. By asserting the social and sharable nature of practical and tacit knowledge, we take off the blindfold and plan our actions. But we do so without certainty and not from some presumed 'overview' from on high, and always with an approximate understanding of the consequences, which we can strive to deepen.

The words of a leader of the Brazilian Workers' Party (PT) in its radically democratic early days – 'the Berlin Wall did not fall on us' – express a similar belief in the possibility of a left politics beyond the fall of the Soviet bloc.[6] The recent social movements of the Western and South American left, and the parties that some of them helped to found, created distinctively participatory forms of democracy, sharing knowledge for a common purpose, without any presumption of certainty or centralized authority. In other words, these social movements – the women's, workers' and green movements most notably – *valued and sought to share tacit and practical knowledge.* They challenged both the presumption that the state knows best and also the 'expertise' of corporate management. But while the free-market right saw tacit knowledge as individual, the social movements worked on the basis that it could be shared, socialized, pooled, exchanged, and could become the basis of alternative forms of expertise and of collaboration for a common purpose, supplemented by other kinds of knowledge – theoretical, historical, statistical – in order to understand fully structures of oppression and develop strategies to overcome them. Hence, I use 'tacit' and 'practical' interchangeably as descriptions of the often invisible knowledge produced, exercised and enhanced in the course of everyday social life and labour. I use 'practical knowledge' because collaborative creativity involves – by the very process of sharing – some kind of articulation of intuition, skill or other tacit form of knowledge, even though often through means other than documentation or centralized information.

Socializing practical knowledge as a source of power

The way in which many social movements of the late 1960s and 1970s organized themselves to enable all members to share and reflect on their experiences, including emotions and feelings, pool their capacities, act together and then consider what they had collectively achieved, is effectively about creating an autonomous source of transformative power. The experience- and practical knowledge-based nature of this power makes it different from the traditional power of the state, which is founded, more often than not, on a statistical knowledge of the overview.

In the practice of these movements, the different sources of power were not necessarily in opposition. Social movements such as the women's movement and radical shop stewards' committees sought political allies to deploy the specific, enabling powers of the state, in order to release the potential power they had created through their own forms of organization. For example, women's groups collaborated to develop community nurseries or childcare centres and then campaigned for public funding to make them more sustainable and provide for more children. Shop stewards' committees drew up proposals for how their members' skills could be usefully deployed, rather than discarded as 'redundant', but they needed public investment or government action for these plans to have any chance of being realized.

To understand fully the significance of these different sources of power, it would help to distinguish two forms of power. Each can be involved in processes or strategies for change. Each is distinctive and unavailable to the other separately.

A New Politics of Knowledge

Rethinking power

On the one hand, there is 'power over', which could also be described as 'power-as-domination'. It involves an asymmetry between those with power and those over whom power is exercised. On the other hand, there is 'power to', or 'power-as-transformative-capacity'. This is the power discovered by social movements of students, radical workers and feminists, for example, as they move beyond protest to creating, in the here and now, practical, prefigurative solutions to current problems.

Historically, social democratic and communist parties have been built around – at best – a benevolent version of the understanding of power-as-domination. Their strategies have been based on winning the power to govern and then steering the state apparatus to meet what they identify as the needs of the people. It is a paternalistic political methodology, which has often involved a low estimation of people's capabilities by the experts responsible for policy making. Beatrice Webb, the Fabian leader who influenced the public-ownership plans of the Labour Party, expressed this starkly when she said of herself and her husband Sidney, and doubtless other Fabian thinkers: 'We have little faith in the "average sensual man". We do not believe that he can do much more than describe his grievances, we do not think he can prescribe his remedies . . . We wish to introduce the professional expert.'[7]

Even Beatrice Webb, however, was shocked by the attitude towards manual workers of one of these experts, William Beveridge, who was responsible for the social security policies at the heart of the welfare state. In her diary entry for 11 August 1940, she describes, approvingly, Beveridge's realization that, if 'the industrial state of Great Britain is to be saved from decay, *planned production and consumption* has to be undertaken' (original emphasis). She continues, less approvingly: 'But as of old, Beveridge is obstinately convinced that he and his class had to do the job, and the trade unionists have to be ignored and the wage-earner ordered to work; the where, when and how, to be settled by a civil servant, with or without a profit-making employer as intermediary. He agrees that there must be a revolution in the economic structure of society; but it must be guided by persons with knowledge and training – i.e. by himself and those he chooses as colleagues.'

Webb, by contrast, believed that workers' consent and co-operation could only be attained 'through some social institution such as trade unionism'.[8] Even so, she clearly did not imagine that trade unions could do much more than bargain over the wages and conditions for this consent and co-operation.

Webb does not comment on another expert responsible for the policies of the 1945 Labour government and the post-war settlement more generally: John Maynard Keynes. But, on his own admission, his attitude was similar to Beveridge's. At a speech to the Liberal summer school in 1925, he summarized why he would not join the Labour Party:

> What is the real repulsion which keeps me away from Labour? There are differences between the several parties in the degree to which the party machine is democratised through and through and the preparation of the party programme democratised in its details. In this respect, the Conservative Party is in much the best position. The inner ring of the party can almost dictate the details and the technique of policy. Traditionally the management of the Liberal Party was also sufficiently autocratic [though Keynes complains of recent pressures to democratize it]. . . .
>
> The Labour Party, on the other hand, is in a far weaker position. I do not believe that the

intellectual elements in the party will ever exercise
adequate control; too much will always be decided
by those who do not know *at all* what they are talking about [original emphasis].[9]

These attitudes do not discredit the important social
and economic ideas of these men and women. There
are many policy ideas that do not in their essential
design require the tacit and practical knowledge of
the 'average sensual man [or woman]' (public ownership of infrastructure would be an example, and
also a redistributive insurance system). However,
when electoral victory leads to implementation,
the institutions through which such policies are
developed to improve people's lives, the everyday
practical knowledge – including the tacit knowledge
and feelings – of the people whose quality of life is
at stake, are essential.

Indeed, the Labour Party's original Clause 4,
with its constitutional commitment to public ownership of the commanding heights of the economy,
implicitly recognized the importance of drawing on
the knowledge of everyday life in its commitment to
'the best obtainable system of popular administration and control of each industry or service'. This,
however, has never even begun to be implemented
systematically – though there have been numerous

local initiatives, both through and independently of the Labour Party. With a political culture shaped by the attitudes we have just described, we can see why it has remained only a paper commitment.

The origins of the notion of power-as-transformative-capacity grew partly out of a widespread frustration with the workings of power-as-domination exercised by political parties of the traditional left. The distinctive emphasis of the rebellions of the 1960s and 1970s – to reappear with the alter-globalization movements of the late 1990s and early 2000s – was that students, shop-floor workers, radical women and others took power into their own hands, discovering through collective action that they had their own capacity to bring about change.

These were not simply pressure groups, demanding with extra militancy that a governing party do something on their behalf. Their approach was directly transformative, including in and against the institutions of the welfare state – educational institutions, in particular.[10] For example, women took action directly to change their relations with men, with each other and with public services; workers took militant action in their workplaces not only to improve their working conditions but also to extend control over the purpose of their labour; and community groups squatted in empty buildings, occupied land against speculation, and campaigned for alternative land-use policies. They no longer focused primarily on the parliamentary politics of representation.

A common theme of these rebellions involved overturning conventional deference to authority and the forms of knowledge deployed by those in authority as a source of legitimacy. Alongside this rejection was a pervasive and self-confident assertion of people's own practical knowledge, as well as their collaborative capacity, against the claims of those in authority to know 'what is best' or 'what needs to be done'. Together with this self-confidence in their transformative abilities went inventiveness about the forms of organization that would build that capacity. While acknowledging the mixed and uneven legacy of the 1960s and 1970s, a distinctive feature of these radical movements was their tendency to emphasize the valuing and sharing of different kinds of knowledge – practical and experiential as well as theoretical and historical.

In their refusal to defer to authority, such movements broke the unspoken bond between knowledge and authority – the idea that those in power know what is best for the mass. In practice, the uncertain, experimental process of democratizing knowledge tends to involve an emphasis on decentralized and networked organizations sharing and developing knowledge horizontally and breaking from models that presume an expert leadership and a more-or-less ignorant membership. It also emphasizes the importance of popular education of the kind developed in Brazil by Paulo Freire, with its stress on nurturing the capacities and creativity that people already exercise in their daily lives.[11] The radically democratic approaches to knowledge pioneered in the 1960s and 1970s (most notably by feminists, but also by networks of workplace and community organizations), along with forms developed by social and indigenous movements, particularly in Latin America, have influenced the organizational and cultural foundations of many civic movements since, from the alter-globalization movement of the late 1990s through to Occupy and the *Indignados*.[12]

In many diverse locations, grassroots trade union and community alliances have been a driving force in democratizing public services or utilities in the face of privatization, but without defending the old hierarchical, paternalistic models. They have become a means of sharing knowledge and building transformative power, both to defend public resources and to democratize and improve the quality of public services. They have shown that they can strengthen citizens' resilience in the face of policies that threaten their material security, offering a degree of autonomy and control that would not otherwise be available to them. And, ultimately, by illustrating in daily practice that there are alternatives, the realization of which lies largely with people themselves, they have often become an important part of strategies for political hegemony.

In this way, power-as-transformative-capacity has begun to produce an institutional infrastructure in many spheres of life – for example, around the production and supply of energy and food, open software, and social and environmentally positive housing – that is distinct from the institutions of representation, with an autonomous source of power in the social organization of practical knowledge. However, it has also become very clear from developing new institutions through social and labour movements that the autonomy of non-state sources of power tends to be precarious and difficult to sustain. This has repeatedly raised the question of how far, and under what conditions, power-as-domination (essentially, in today's context: having control over state institutions) can be a resource for power-as-transformative-capacity.

It is important to recognize that, although there is a sharp distinction between these two types of power, they are not necessarily counterposed in practice. We must therefore probe further into how political institutions need to change for power-as-domination to be an enabling resource, and to provide support for power-as-transformative-capacity, as distinct from weakening or overwhelming originally autonomous forms of social power, as is so often the case. We also need to ask what kinds of transformative capacity are strategically relevant to bringing about change, with or without the resource of power-as-domination.

The perspective of a long revolution towards self-government

Raymond Williams' *The Long Revolution*[13] provides an appropriately historical perspective on this. He seeks to understand 'the rising determination, almost everywhere, that people should govern themselves'. He considers this to be a lengthy, difficult and complex but 'genuine revolution; transforming men and institutions; continually extended and deepened by the actions of millions, continually and variously opposed by explicit reaction and by the pressure of habitual forms and ideas'.

Williams' focus is on the actions of millions – not

as 'the masses' to be captured and led as objects of power but as subjects aspiring to determine their own futures. He documents how they do so in many different ways, fetishizing none as more 'revolutionary' than others. Thus, the millions who voted Labour in 1945, determined that there would be no return to the pre-war conditions of extreme inequality and mass deprivation, moved the long revolution forward. Through their confidence at having effectively won the war against fascism, they kept the Labour government to its promise to create, after a gruelling few years, a decent life for the returning heroes. By the 1960s, the time at which he was writing, Williams said that the 'most useful service already performed by the new genera-tion is its challenge to society to compare its ideals and its practice'.

I share Williams' starting point: the rising desire for self-government. This is at the heart of the politics of knowledge. His analysis of the period from 1945 to the 1960s enables me to reflect on a dilemma about the 1945 government and its after-math, at the same time illustrating the complexity of the 'long revolution': the ebbs and flows of the rising desire for self-government and the difficul-ties in creating the institutions through which to realize it.

A New Politics of Knowledge

The dilemma is this. The 1945 government made social reforms, definitively from the centre, engineered by the kind of expert knowledge described by Beatrice Webb and rebuffing any suggestions of popular participation in shaping the new institutions of the welfare state and the nationalized infrastructure. So how, at the same time, did it pave the way, through the expansion of education and the spread of means of communication, for the pervasive and widespread desire for participatory forms of self-government that burst into public view with the rebellious movements of the late 1960s?

The collective confidence and militant hope behind Labour's victory

The answer I reconstruct – Williams does not address this question explicitly – is that Labour's victory in 1945 was a powerful but contained expression of the desire for self-government, which, for all its force to bring immediate change, failed to create new common institutions of self-government. The Cold War and the economic and cultural hold of a McCarthyite USA over British politics made sure of that. The 1945 government did begin, however, to change the lives of working people in ways that stimulated and enabled the desire and capacity for self-government to grow. This was evident largely beneath the institutional surface, created by working people through relations of mutuality using the resources of these public institutions. We saw the extraordinary energies generated by the experience of working people having won the war flooding into the old institutions of the Labour Party and the British parliamentary system, putting them under pressure to reform daily life beyond recognition. In this way, one could argue that the achievements of the 1945 government were as much a matter of popular will as of elite expertise.

In that sense, and because of the nature of the improvements made, the 1945 government marked an important early step in the long revolution. This was not because it produced new self-governing institutions – though Aneurin Bevan, the main architect of the National Health Service (NHS), was influenced by his own experience of a long-standing organization of this kind in his home town of Tredegar.[14] Rather, the 1945 government left memories, direct and transmitted, and produced changes in the lives of those who, as the generation who matured in the 1960s, would become impatient for genuine democratic control.

The conditions of an anti-fascist war produced

a remarkable radicalization and self-confidence among working-class people, whether serving in the armed forces or engaged in wartime production. The demands of war had required the ruling coalition to undertake an unprecedented exercise in planning – not only military, but also social and economic. This state intervention had provided the indispensable conditions of victory. Moreover, the millions of people who were fighting on the frontline were assured that the state would guarantee them employment, security, welfare, housing and educational opportunity. These people assumed these conditions as their right, not as acts of paternalistic benevolence. They campaigned for a Labour government with all the self-confidence of those responsible for defeating a fascist enemy and determined not to return to the conditions of 1930s peace – unemployment, poverty, slum housing.

This self-confidence was politicized through extensive and rare levels of discussion and education during the daily life of the war. Ralph Miliband describes how 'in barracks and mess decks, in factories and air raid shelters, in organized and even more in unorganized debates and discussions, leftists of anti-fascist Popular Front days found an audience receptive as never before to the message of socialist change'.[15] At the same time, the confidence of organized labour was on the rise as the bargaining power of workers' shop-floor organizations benefited from the full employment created by the war.

After describing the huge upsurge of (mainly unofficial) strikes in 1945, Lewis Minkin, a meticulous analyst of the labour movement and the 'contentious alliance' between trade unions and the Labour Party, sums up how this 'mainly covert but intense pattern of industrial conflict reflected both an increased confidence of working people and the growth of a more vigorous industrial Left'.[16] This trade union strength produced an unprecedented level of collaboration in the government cabinet and a massive increase in trade union affiliation.

As Minkin says, government policies implemented Labour Party conference resolutions as never before or since. But, despite this increase in power over macro policy, there were no concessions to union radicals, who were pressing for a role for trade unionists in the day-to-day control of the nationalized industries. Many bosses of the former private companies became managing directors when the government took ownership.

'There is not yet a very large number of workers in Britain capable of taking over large enterprises', declared Sir Stafford Cripps, a past leader of the party's left, at one point expelled for his links with Communist Party campaigns, and speaking as President of the Board of Trade to the Trade Union Congress (TUC) in 1946. 'I think', he concluded – illustrating an elitism that persisted among the more upper-class leaders of the Labour left – 'it would be almost impossible to have worker-controlled industry in Britain, even if it were on the whole desirable'.[17]

The fact that workers' control was even being debated was an indication that these were extraordinary times. And although things were soon to revert to normal, the changes brought about in these years in the daily lives and prospects of working people strengthened the rising desire for self-government, which gathered momentum beneath the outwardly functioning appearance of the old institutions.

Despite this, the emerging Cold War worked to subdue debate and counter pressure on the later years of the Attlee government by marginalizing and demonizing the left, while financial and political pressures began to close in on the post-war Labour government, dampening the high hopes of millions of those who supported it. At the same time, pragmatic trade union leaders, led by Ernest Bevin, consolidated the Labour Party rules that separated industrial and political concerns and deferred to the autonomy of the parliamentary party, inhibiting any tendency for workplace militancy to overflow into politics, but securing a place for national officials in corporatist arrangements that began to be created by Conservative as well as Labour governments, building on tripartite arrangements – government, business and the unions – set up during the war.[18]

The Labour Party returned to its parliamentarist identity with a stronger loyalism and tribalism than before as a result of the determination both to maintain its position as a party of government and to avoid the cross-party compromises of Ramsay MacDonald. By the 1950 general election, the Labour government's main concerns were to dispel any idea that the Labour Party was – heaven forbid – 'fellow travelling' with the Communist Party; to demonstrate that Labour accepted the 'mixed economy' and would propose no further inroads into the private sector; and to attract the middle-class vote whose seduction had already become an obsession with Labour's electoral strategists.[19]

The transformation of Labour into a party that could make possible 'popular administration and control' depended, then, on a mass level of radicalization, perhaps unreplicable beyond wartime. Such radicalization also needed movements both inside and outside the Labour Party. This was provided in the mid-1940s by the activists of the anti-fascist Popular Front and the growing membership of not only the Communist Party (whose attitude to popular participation and the democratization of knowledge would often – at a leadership level, at any rate – be hostile) but also the independent-left Commonwealth Party. Such a radicalization could not be catalysed simply from inside the party. Nothing quite like it has occurred since.

It's when all's quiet that the seed's a-growing

By the late 1950s, however, a 'new left' was emerging, mainly among the intelligentsia broadly defined – media professionals and self-educated working-class intellectuals, as well as academics – that rejected both sides of the Cold War. It was 1956, with Soviet tanks on the streets of Budapest and British ships and troops in the Suez Canal, that was the catalyst. One of the new left's most eloquent early voices was E. P. Thompson. With the instincts of the social historian, he was attentive to what was happening beneath the surface of the institutions of the Cold War. While the international show of the Stalinist Soviet bloc versus NATO and the capitalist West proceeded, he noticed the young people who had slunk out of the theatre to make their own music on the streets. Prompted by 'the positives of Aldermaston and the negatives of '"hip" and the "beats"', he spied a new critical temper. It offered a future outside the political culture shaped by the Cold War. 'Beneath the polarisation of power and ideology in the Cold War world', he wrote, 'a new, rebellious human nature was being formed, just as the new grass springs up beneath the snow'.[20]

In *The Making of the English Working Class*, Thompson, writing of the 1820s in a comparable period of retreat and defeat and mild prosperity, quotes a London artisan alerting nineteenth-century historian Henry Mayhew: 'People fancy that when all's quiet that all's stagnating. Propaganda is going on for all that. It's when all's quiet that the seed's a-growing. Republicans and Socialists are pressing their doctrines.'[21]

The quiet decades of the 1950s and early 1960s were the years in which workers' strength and organization in the workplace began to grow, benefiting from the bargaining power of the economic boom and creating the conditions for an increasingly militant workplace trade unionism, with some autonomy from the alliance of trade union leaders with the parliamentary Labour Party (PLP); years in which networked activists against the nuclear bomb converged to create the Aldermaston Marches, through which, every Easter weekend, over 50,000 marchers from all parts of the left and dissenting opinion created a radical left politics independent of political parties (though periodically engaging with it) and a space in which politics and culture came together creatively and experimentally – even renewing, through the Committee of 100 and the campaign against regional seats of post-nuclear government, the tradition of direct action.[22] They were years in which film-makers documented everyday working-class life, its ingenuity and its forms of cultural rebellion; in which Simone de Beauvoir's *Second Sex* gave women marginalized by domesticity and subordinated by Hollywood culture the confidence to experiment with autonomy and ways of living that refused male domination; in which popular music provided a language for escaping the narrow constraints of conventional values and morals. Fertile ground, then, for the burgeoning new left which was, in its own way, searching to theorize both the failures and defeats of the Russian Revolution and the limits of Labourism.

By the end of the 1960s, and most visibly in the rebellions of 1968, a new consciousness was emerging among the generation that did not itself experience the war, that benefited from the material advantages and expanded educational opportunities of the welfare state and, as if echoing their victorious forebears, expected something more than material security. In different ways, they demanded democratic control and, drawing on the new traditions of direct action, took autonomous initiatives to achieve it, whether as students, workers, women, tenants, or civic activists more generally. In particular, the bond between knowledge and authority, which was at the centre of the benevolent paternalism of the post-war settlement, was in their sights and began to be broken.

Moreover, the new contradictions – distinctive to post-war capitalism – posed problems to which the previous nostrums of socialism, as it was known then, also had no adequate answer: socialism had become rather vague and confused after the experiences of communism and the nationalizations of the Attlee government. So these were also years of searching, questioning and experimenting with alternatives in the here and now, rather than promoting a ready-made programme.

It was not until 1973 that anything remotely comparable with the levels of self-confidence and radicalization seen in the 1940s flowed through the institutions of the Labour Party again. At that time, it was a result of wider economic and social processes rather than inner-party dynamics. Debates within the Labour Party followed the impact of the growing self-confidence, expectations and militancy of shop-floor trade unionism, together with the reverberations of the anti-colonial liberation movements, the events of 1968 and the assertive rebellions of the first post-war generation as students, women, gay people, black people and other subordinated groups. They wanted more than the material security they had come to take for granted and were seeking to transform the power relations towards which they no longer had deference.

In this spirit, the Labour Party was contingently – and, as it turned out for many, temporarily – a host to many of these energies. They shaped the initiatives of Tony Benn and Ken Livingstone. But the energy and creativity were generated autonomously, and loyalty to the Labour Party was not these activists' overriding concern.

This brings us to the extraordinary victory of Jeremy Corbyn as Labour Party leader in 2015. Again, the energies of the movement that propelled him to office came primarily from outside the Labour Party. They came from environmental campaigners and direct action groups, those motivated by inequality, austerity and the 2008 financial crash, and from thousands of trade union members radicalized by austerity and what it meant for their living standards, public services and the prospects for young people. Jeremy Corbyn was no Tony Benn, although his political development had taken place through his thirty-year collaboration with Benn and the Socialist Campaign Group of MPs. Whereas Benn championed radical change through his charisma and established status as a leading politician, Corbyn symbolized a new effort to open the party to becoming a movement for radical change through his very modesty and daily support for others in struggle.

Alex Nunns, author of the most authoritative description of Jeremy Corbyn's 'improbable path to power', comments that this participatory ethos, rather than the specific detail of policies, 'was really the essence of Corbyn's entire campaign. For disempowered party members in particular, it was the reason Corbyn was so appealing. He was offering them empowerment, and there was no mistaking the message – every aspect of Corbyn's candidacy, from his own selfless demeanour to the specific form of rail nationalisation he was proposing, was about inviting people to take part.'[23]

What is striking about Jeremy Corbyn, and makes him different from other European leaders of the radical left – often called 'left populist' – is that his appeal is not centred on himself as a charismatic leader. It is based on an invitation to join an urgent crusade for a new politics based on popular participation. His promise is to invite people to participate in developing the policies that the government he seeks to lead would implement. He is not a left populist in the sense of being a leader in whom the people are encouraged to invest their faith, against the elite. His appeal has been his encouragement to people to have confidence in themselves.

As if explaining this demeanour, Corbyn describes his personal attitude to 'expertise': 'I never held in awe those who have had higher education', he has said, nor did he have 'a sense of superiority over those who don't. Life is life. Some of the wisest people you meet are sweeping our streets.'[24]

My argument is not that new politics stands or falls by Jeremy Corbyn. Rather, I will illustrate what a new politics has meant in practice through looking at grassroots initiatives that overturn the traditional hierarchies of knowledge and authority, and in doing so overcome the division between economics and politics, which has become increasingly deep as the welfare state and other forms of visible state involvement in the economy have been dismantled. My intention, having described the material and cultural creativity that has been emerging beneath the political class, is to take this 'new politics' seriously and to ask what political institutions, of state, party and economy, would be like if the practical knowledge of working and would-be-working people were built into their decision-making.

I will draw lessons from disappointing international experiences (for example in Brazil and, more recently, Greece) in which I initially placed much hope because of their recognition of the capacities of 'ordinary' people and their attempts to build this recognition into their foundations as political organizations. When they faced the problems of winning office and then actually governing, in the face of hostile forces, these organizations – the Brazilian Workers' Party (PT) and the Greek radical coalition and later governing party Syriza, in particular[25] – proved unable to build sufficient transformative power independently of the old political institutions. They failed to escape these institutions' weighty power, reinforced by the constraints of the corporate global market and its policing institutions, most notably the International Monetary Fund (IMF) and the European Central Bank (ECB).

Many of the founders and original leading activists of these movement-based parties were seriously

committed to popular participation and the sharing of power on the basis of a strong belief in
cultural equality with their supporters. They had
proclaimed a strong belief in people's capacity for
self-government. The pull of office and the pressures of hostile forces, however, proved too great
to resist, and in neither Brazil nor Greece did they
have sufficiently strong roots in society to develop
independent sources of transformative power.

The development of a new politics, rooted in a
new economics, will often be independent of any
one political party, and expressed in municipal
alliances and in different left and left green parties at various levels. The aim must be both the
spread of the present cells of such new institutions
and the emergence of political leaders who will
reverse Beatrice Webb's statement and instead say
clearly: 'We value the fact that so-called "ordinary"
men and women can not only point to their problems but can also, through collaboration, produce
positive solutions. Let us develop with them the
institutions and resources that could enable them to
do so' – and mean it.

2

The New Politics in Practice

The possibilities of new institutions are usually an outcome of the conjuncture of new ideas and mentalities – including a crisis in old ideas – and a shift in the balance of political and/or economic power.

In this chapter, I look at four examples of where the changes in understandings of knowledge described in chapter 1, arising from the breakdown of the bond between authority and knowledge – and, with it, the assertion by rebellious movements of previously marginalized tacit and practical knowledge – converged with changes in economic and political power to demonstrate a new economic logic based on producing for social use rather than for profitable exchange. I explore an example from three of the four main sectors of the economy – manufacturing, public administration and communications (the fourth being the domestic or household economy). I also indicate the wider transformation to which these initiatives aspire, were their innovations to spread and to gain political support.

Economic initiatives based on the sharing of tacit knowledge

The first example concerns a group of well-organized manufacturing and design engineers in Lucas Aerospace, a subsidiary of the large, originally UK-based corporation, Lucas Industries Ltd. When the management decided to close some factories and cut jobs in others, declaring the workers 'redundant', the shop stewards' combine committee challenged the company with an alternative plan. In the process, this workplace organization became a means of sharing workers' tacit knowledge to produce a socially useful alternative plan, based on prototypes of actual product designs. They were appalled at management's presumption that their skills were 'redundant', when all around them they could see urgent social needs concerning health, disability, public transport, renewable energy and energy conservation – to name but a few – for which they could design and manufacture useful products. They rejected the idea that technology was value-neutral and unquestionable and insisted that all choices concerning it were based on implicit social values.

The second example illustrates a similar methodology of sharing workers' knowledge through a participatory workplace trade unionism involved in the administration of municipal public services. It concerns council workers in Newcastle, faced with the threat of privatization, who believed that their direct, practical knowledge of the sources of inefficiency in the services they provided was of far more public value than the solutions proposed by the private company, British Telecom, bidding to take over the council's information technology (IT) and related services. Like the Lucas Aerospace workers, they turned their workplace union into a means of sharing tacit knowledge. With members in every department, they had an inside view of the administration's flows and processes that was in many ways superior to that of management, clouded as it was by departmental empire-building and protective silos. This local branch of Unison was able to make its democratization of knowledge the basis of a reform of the council's administration that saw more than £11 million savings reallocated to frontline services, including care for the elderly.

Lastly, I report on work being done by a new generation of knowledge producers – and would-be democratizers of knowledge – using digital technologies to share knowledge as a basis of creating value for the common good.

Each experience illustrates different kinds of cellular structures of a hybrid economy whose common logic is the collaborative creation of social value rather than the alienated production of exchange value. In the following chapter, I will explore the kind of systems, equivalent in some senses to the human nervous system, through which such cells might be co-ordinated or interconnected.

Sharing tacit knowledge in manufacturing: Lucas Aerospace

Back in the 1970s, with British industry contracting and unemployment rising, workers at the arms-manufacturing company Lucas Aerospace came up with a pioneering plan to retain jobs by proposing alternative, socially useful applications of the company's technology and their own skills. The 'Lucas Plan' remains one of the most radical and forward-thinking attempts ever made by workers to gain power over the purpose of production and demonstrate, in practice, a democratic direction for industrial change.

Forty years later, we are facing a convergence of crises: militarism and nuclear weapons, climate chaos, and the destruction of jobs by new technologies and automation. These crises mean we have to start thinking about technology as inherently political, as the Lucas Aerospace workers did, and about knowledge and enlightened common sense being characteristics of workers and so-called 'ordinary' citizens as much as of civil servants and politicians – if not more so. A new generation of young activists, working for peace and for a transition to a low-carbon economy, are reopening the debate about industrial conversion and economic democracy.

Democratic egalitarianism

What so inspires me about the Lucas Plan is the democratic egalitarianism running through its every part – the work processes, the products and even the very technology they propose.

Here, Laurence Hall was explaining how this egalitarian ethic inspired him to make 'the Lucas Plan' the focus of a regular gathering of Young Quakers in Lancaster, up the road from the Trident nuclear submarine yards in Barrow. Eurig Scandrett, from the Scottish Green Party, similarly made 'the Lucas Plan' the theme for Green Party trade unionists at their annual conference, because 'it is the most inspiring example of workers on the shop floor who get self-organised and demand to make what humanity needs'. The fact that the plan was defeated does not render its insights irrelevant, or dilute its capacity to inspire.

The broad outline of the Lucas Aerospace workers' story is a familiar one: workers faced redundancies, got organized, resisted, and insisted that their skills and machinery were not 'redundant'. But they went further. They drew together alternative ideas along with those of supportive academics and, with the encouragement of Tony Benn (then Industry Secretary in the Labour government), produced their 'Alternative Corporate Plan for Socially Useful Production', illustrated with prototypes. Management refused to negotiate. The government, under pressure from the Confederation of British Industry (CBI) and the City, made gestures of a willingness to talk but would not make any move that management did not approve. The plan was never implemented by Lucas Aerospace, although commercial companies elsewhere, such as in Germany, picked up some of the ideas.

So what lessons can we draw from this experience of 'ordinary' people organizing and sharing their practical knowledge and skills to produce a viable plan for socially useful production? Some of the main ones are discussed below.

- *Lesson 1 Find common ground*
  A first condition for this group of fairly conventional, mainly middle-aged, male trade unionists to create what became a beacon of an alternative economics for future generations was the building of the organization that eventually provided the means for many individual intelligences to become effectively 'collective'. Faced with the divide-and-rule of corporate 'rationalization', they could well have ended up at each other's throats, competing for the few jobs that remained. But, through an ethic of honesty and mutual respect they built the shared trust and everyday democracy to remain united and creative.

  The shop stewards across the Lucas Aerospace sites forged collective strength over a decade of taking action on basic common issues such as wages and conditions. This served to unite groups of workers with very different traditions and interests. Fundamental to the culture of the combine committee was its belief in the capacities of its members on the shop floor and in the offices. As Mike Cooley – one of the combine's diverse leaders and an international authority on human-centred, computer-based systems – put it, after stressing the importance of tacit knowledge as an intuitive sense of what is to be done: 'I do not counterpose tacit knowledge, intuition or know-how against analytic thinking; rather I believe that a holistic organisation and work process is one which provides the correct balance between analytical thinking and intuition.'[1] In a sense, the process of developing the plan itself attempted to create just such a holistic work process, overcoming the fragmentation and de-skilling of both twentieth-century Taylorism[2] and the computer technologies of the future.

- *Lesson 2 Build democracy*
  Immense care and collective self-reflectiveness were needed to bring such diverse groups into a relatively united organization, and to ensure that the insights arising from workers' varied experiences gained expression and synergy through the combine committee.

All thirty-five (or so) delegates had the right to speak at meetings of the multi-union committee, but decisions on recommendations were taken back to the workforce on the basis of 'one site (or factory), one vote'. The decisions were binding on the delegates, who were expected to campaign for them at their local sites, where members were free to accept or reject them as they thought best. This consciously and sensitively protected relationship between the combine and the different factories made it feel as though the members and local shop stewards were 'absent friends', whose presence at combine meetings was palpable.

- *Lesson 3 Build alliances and look ahead*
  Although the combine won victories on wages and conditions in the years before the plan, when it came to jobs they felt as though they were engaged in a labour of Sisyphus. They would win a local agreement to halt job losses, only to find that jobs were being slashed in different places through the decisions not of local but of central management.

  The problem was Lucas' centralized restructuring towards longer production runs and more computer-controlled machinery, and its shifting investment in other European countries and the USA. The traditional approach of the trade union movement, based on regional structures and national officials without significant direct involvement of workplace organization, proved inadequate, so the combine produced its own experts and made use of outside help to educate and prepare itself.

- *Lesson 4 Building collective strategic intelligence* 'We're in a situation where politics is unavoidable', the combine executive argued in *Combine News*, in response to rumours of nationalization of part of the aerospace industry. 'Though there have been problems with nationalisation, we could, with the full involvement of all our members, insist on adequate safeguards against many of these. The advantages would be considerable, we would finally be working for our ultimate employers.'[3]

  They went on to sow the seeds of the alternative plan: 'We could insist that the skill and talents of our members could be used to the full to engage in socially useful products like monorails and hovercraft, and to ensure that these skills are used in a much truer sense in the interests of the nation as a whole.'

This led to the presentation of the case for the nationalization of Lucas Aerospace to Tony Benn, then Secretary of State for Industry. He was impressed: 'Here was a group who had done the work to anticipate the problem. Others had come to me at the last minute saying their firm had gone bust and what could I do.'[4]

For all his enthusiasm, Benn lacked the power to agree to nationalization, but suggested that the combine draw up an alternative corporate strategy.

At first there was some scepticism. But the necessity of finding a new solution drove them on, and beyond management's framework. They challenged the profit motive of the company and talked in terms of social benefit. This was the basis on which they drew up an alternative plan.

The process of drawing this up was a challenge to old habits and ways of thinking. 'The combine wanted to know what machine tools we had. To do the corporate plan we were having to think as if we were planning. It really made the shop stewards sit up', remembers Mick Cooney, a fitter from Burnley. The combine asked site committees questions aimed to stimulate workers' imagination: 'How could the plant be run by the workforce? Are there any socially useful products which your plant could design and manufacture?'

The stimulus of experiences of all kinds, of problems facing the community as much as ideas coming from the workplace, led to 150 product ideas in six categories: medical equipment, transport vehicles, improved braking systems, energy conservation, oceanics and telechiric machines.

- *Lesson 5 Know the limits*
  The Lucas workers' plan for socially useful production as an alternative to job loss inspired workers throughout the defence-related engineering industry. This included the vast yards building nuclear submarines in Barrow, where designers submitted alternatives to the Labour Party defence policy committee in the mid-1970s. At this time, the yards were owned by Vickers Ltd, which also made tanks at the Elswick works on the Tyne in Newcastle.

  In Vickers, a strong combine committee had been built in response to pressures of rationalization, acquisitions and closures very similar to those that had stimulated the growth of the Lucas Aerospace combine. Both had links with the Institute for Workers' Control (IWC) and, through its conferences and political connections, they found common cause in the idea of alternative plans for socially constructive production. The shop stewards in the Elswick and Scotwood works responded to threats of redundancies by drawing up such plans and gaining the support of Tony Benn and his team. The Tyneside Vickers stewards made contact with shop stewards at Barrow, especially in the design office, who were already doing their own work on alternatives. In Barrow, there had been an earlier initiative towards diversification from Vickers management, led by an innovative engineer, George Henson, whose Quaker principles caused him to refuse to work on the (eventually cancelled) TSR2 reconnaissance aircraft at Vickers' Weybridge plant. This had prompted his move to Barrow, where management wanted to diversify from total dependence on government defence contracts.

However, Vickers responded to subsequent nationalization plans by keeping the profitable diversified section, making submersibles for deep-sea oil exploration, and handing over the yards dealing with military orders to the government. The separation of the two production processes was a major blow to any longer-term diversification programme. Its brief success under Henson, however, proved a powerful memory and lesson for the designers who were still working on nuclear submarines, and they were responsive to the contacts from Vickers' shop stewards on the Tyne suggesting collaboration on alternative plans to submit to the Labour Party's diversification committee.[5]

Labour's defeat in the 1979 election closed down these possibilities. In the 1980s, however, some of the designers helped to create the Barrow Alternative Employment Committee (BAEC) to propose alternatives to Trident. By this time, following privatization, the Barrow yards were owned by British Aerospace (BAe), which rejected the strategy of keeping skilled teams together through diversification. BAe, a large multinational with freedom to move skilled workers from plant to plant, concentrated entirely on its 'core business' of Trident submarines, whatever the cost in terms of job losses. The only exception was warships, the manufacture of which dominated the yards until the recent renewal of Trident.[6]

Terry McSorley, a member of the now-defunct BAEC, told me: 'The lesson I learnt is that site-based diversification won't work.' He argues for an approach that integrates defence conversion with industrial strategy.

Steve Schofield, who was a researcher for the BAEC, draws a similar conclusion: 'The Labour movement needs a much more ambitious arms conversion programme to challenge the embedded power of the military–industrial complex.' He argues for a change in security policy towards UN peacekeeping and peace-building. He suggests a combination of publicly funded national and regional investment banks for industries such as offshore wind and wave power to ensure an equitable distribution that benefits arms-dependent communities, including Barrow-in-Furness, Glasgow, Preston, Aldermaston and Plymouth.

Drawing on Lucas and his own more problematic experience in Barrow, Schofield is certain that trade union and community participation is essential to ensuring that the skills of working people are maintained and enhanced. But it would need to be on an industry-wide basis rather than restricted to a single company.[7]

We are in new times for trade union organization, but interest in democratic economics is increasing with the spread of green and solidarity economies, commons-based peer-to-peer production, and grassroots fabrication in 'hackerspaces' and 'fab labs'. These developments have deepened ideas about connecting tacit knowledge and participatory prototyping to the political economy of technology development, as was the case with Lucas.

The experience of the Lucas plan offers lessons for Labour's proposed Arms-Conversion Agency. In particular, it suggests elements of a methodology for a network of organizations with an understanding of technological development not as an autonomous and value-neutral process, but as shaped by social choices – choices that the Lucas stewards showed need to become democratic.

This 'ordinary' group of workers gave a glimpse of how it might be possible to create the foundations of a democratic economy. It is such workers, after all, who have the practical know-how on which technological development depends. The problem is how to realize, and provide support and a platform for, such capacity. That includes a leading role for government, but on a collaborative basis – the opposite from that envisaged by the Webbs (see chapter 1), as an expert alternative to the 'average sensual man' unable to produce 'positive prescriptions' of their own.

The democratization of knowledge as a basis of public service reform: Newcastle Unison's successful struggle for a democratic alternative to privatization

If the aspiration of an 'enabling state' is ever to be more than rhetorical, there has to be a transformation, a deep democratization, of public administration itself. The impact of citizen participation in policy making or budget setting (as in 'participatory budgeting'[8]), or the possibility of municipal support for a local social economy, will invariably be blocked if the administration of municipalities remains based on opaque hierarchies that deny power to the frontline staff who have daily knowledge of citizens' needs.

The dominant forms of state administration have been the paternalist technocracy common to social democracy and the 'new public management' (NPM) of neoliberalism. Here, I explore an experience that exemplifies the idea of 'transformative resistance', aiming at democratic public administration. Public-sector workers, in close collaboration with service users and local communities, defended public services by transforming (and improving) them.

The New Politics in Practice

'Transformative resistance': An illustrative case

In 1999, the Newcastle City Council IT workers, organized through the council branch of the public services workers' union, Unison, began a struggle not only to protect their IT services but to fight for the workplace democracy necessary to improve them. The branch leadership wanted to win popular support for their resistance to privatization by showing that the union was concerned not only with its members' workplace interests but also with the public interest. The union involved its members in proposing, disseminating and implementing improvements to municipal services. This example is worth exploring. It points not only to the potential of transformative resistance, but also to the limitations of entirely local campaigns in a country dominated by market politics.[9]

The workers in Newcastle's IT services process and deliver the council's key revenue streams, such as rent and council taxes. They also run the council's exchequer service, which pays invoices, chases debts, administers its payroll and personnel systems, and operates its 'one stop' customer service centres. This infrastructure is central to the council's daily business. But the services were based on expensive and inefficient technology that had never been effectively understood or challenged by elected councillors. Decisions on a radical reorganization of the system were put off and the system patched up, leading to further inefficiencies and what has been described as a 'baroque' technology.[10]

This has been typical of much of the public sector in Britain. The term 'baroque', used originally in this context in the arms sector, can also be applied to the design of administrative systems with their maze-like, buck-passing quality. Although the status quo involves out-of-date technological and organizational systems that are very expensive to maintain and adapt, budgets are usually 'nodded through' by councillors, especially where one party has long-term domination, without any debate or interrogation. They effectively abrogate any responsibility for improving the quality of public services and fail to scrutinize whether public money is being spent in the public's best interests.

It was this fatalistic mentality towards their own procedures that led the Labour leadership of Newcastle City Council to look to the private sector and the idea of a public–private 'joint venture' for the answer. They presumed, following the approach of Tony Blair's New Labour, that a private company would do a more efficient job than they could themselves. British Telecom (BT), a financially troubled corporation in search of profits with minimal risk, put in a bid to be the private-sector partner, with an eye on positioning itself, through no productive capacity or entrepreneurial skill of its own, to win more long-term public-sector contracts in the region. Before the trade unions in the IT section of the council decided to resist, the company had been getting its way with a demoralized municipal management, backed by leading politicians desperate to meet government budgetary targets.

The civic centre branch of Unison had remained politicized throughout the Thatcher years, bucking the general trend in the unions towards depoliticization. Working with a sympathetic, public service-oriented senior management, it had protected local services from Thatcher's 'contracting-out' culture in the 1980s and 1990s by insisting that public services contracts include social clauses. Private companies were rarely able to satisfy these clauses, so in practice little privatization occurred.

The unusually strategic and politically conscious trade unionism of the local union leaders in Newcastle stemmed from the fact that they had not worked exclusively within the council. They also had extensive experience in radical community politics across the city, especially from working with council tenants. With the help of a politically engaged research organization (the European

Services Strategy Unit), they looked at the problem of keeping services public from the standpoint of tenants and the wider society, not just that of public-sector employees concerned with wages and conditions – though the branch, like the Lucas Aerospace combine, had won its credibility with its members by being effective on these basic issues. Its leaders had also built a very participative and politically conscious trade union branch, with a strong emphasis on education and developing the political capacities of younger members.

The branch shop stewards became involved in scrutinizing the details of BT's bid. They quickly realized, in the words of one of them – Lisa Marshall – that: 'Private business did not have any special expertise. As we looked over their bid in a special room provided by BT – we were not allowed to take copies away with us – we found a lot that we knew could be done better.'

Reinforced with this confidence in their own capacity to offer a viable alternative to privatization, Lisa and her colleagues engaged in industrial action and organized massive marches through the city under the banner 'Our City is Not For Sale'. This was intended to awaken Labour politicians to their public responsibilities, and in October 2001 the council's Labour group voted to reject privatization unless all in-house alternatives had been explored. This opened the way for management, with union agreement and participation, to prepare an in-house bid, which was accepted by the council in September 2002.

The union not only blocked the council's attempt to privatize the service, but helped to shape a new public-led strategy for improvement. Its goal was to maximize public benefit, in contrast to BT's goal of maximizing private profit. The shop stewards also had a say in who was appointed to run the new 'City Service' department that was formed to carry out the changes outlined in the successful in-house bid. They negotiated a relationship with the new management that secured their members' interests – most notably, that there would be no compulsory redundancies – and ensured that all problems were solved through discussion and, where necessary, negotiation. Power and initiative were transferred to the frontline staff, with the elimination of layers of hierarchy and supervision. Management was to be organized on the basis of agreement rather than by command.

The contribution of workers to the content of the service was evident in, for example, a new contact centre with an ethos of making a special effort to help people, rather than measuring success simply in terms of the rate at which calls were answered.

The ethos was one of improving efficiency in terms of public benefit by drawing on the workers' shared knowledge and insight. The leading managers believed in the public sector and its employees and the distinctive contribution they could make. 'We shouldn't be mimicking the private sector. We must find ways of being innovative on our own terms, and in closer partnership with service users', as City Service manager Kath Moore puts it. Her belief in the public sector, she explains, 'is founded on the people who work for the public sector. There is so much talent, commitment, energy and passion to get it right for our service users.'[11]

Here is a glimpse, then, of democratic public administration, reaching parts that a purely representative democracy cannot. By recognizing and organizing its members' capacity and practical knowledge, the union branch had pressured politicians and council managers to avoid privatization and commit themselves to an internal process of change and improvement. This was not 'pseudo-participation'. Rather, on this basis, the management and unions embarked on a negotiated strategy of improvement involving all levels of staff at every stage. In effect, City Service instituted a form of day-to-day industrial democracy. Any conflicts would be addressed through collective bargaining. With regard to the role of the unions in these transformations of the service, the department's director says, 'The union made me accountable for the change.'

Net savings from these changes amounted to £228 million over an eleven-year period, which were reallocated to frontline services such as care for the elderly and youth provision. This took place without any enforced redundancies. Instead, the middle-level management whose supervisory jobs were eliminated accepted retraining and voluntary redundancy deals. This acceptance by senior management that no one would be sacked was a condition of the unions' positive involvement in the process.

This is a significant story, though not easily replicated. It is a practical demonstration of an alternative, democracy-driven model for improving the efficiency of public administration. It presents a different option from the market-driven processes that are currently being imposed on the global South, including Southern Europe, under the supposed imperatives of austerity and efficiency.

The new department, City Service, was managed on a relatively democratic basis for several years. Had the Labour group been more understanding and supportive of the process, it could have been spread across the council and given more institutional permanence. As it was, when Labour returned to office in 2011, following a period when they lost control of the council, they marginalized it and the managers responsible. In that year, the union branch was also considerably weakened in its capacity to do more than defending members' jobs and conditions by the death of Kenny Bell, the strategically minded branch leader. His strategy of transformative resistance was not well established in Unison – beyond the regional level – not least because the tasks of simple survival were so tough in the face of both New Labour and then a new Conservative government, elected in 2010, intent on severe austerity and the defeat of public-sector trade unions. This locked Unison's national leadership into a defensive mode that did not allow much space for the principles of the Newcastle model to take root.

Commons peer-to-peer production

Finally, we must explore the distinctive consequences of the revolution in information and communications technology (ICT) for the democratization and sharing of knowledge. Its full implications for a new political economy are still in the process of experimentation and study. The experiences I will point to, mainly in Barcelona, aim, like other examples discussed in this chapter, at producing use value, rather than value to be realized through the capitalist market. And the sharing of knowledge, or information from which people intend to generate knowledge, is – as in the other examples in this chapter – fundamental.

It was appropriate that, in the first decade of the twenty-first century, a new generation should make the tools of this technological revolution their own. In the hands of a generation radicalized at the end of the twentieth century, when deregulated, corporate-driven capitalism and the inequalities and injustices associated with it were at their height, the new technology awakened imaginative and radical visions of new forms of production.

It is appropriate, too, that, half a century on from 1968, these activists took democratization to a more ambitious level. Their parents' generation had challenged the authority of those who claimed to know what was good for them, as students, as women and as citizens, or of those who suppressed their capacities as workers and robbed them of the fruits of their creativity. The generation of the alter-globalization movement of the late 1990s / early 2000s, on the other hand, saw the possibilities opened up by the new ICT for ways of organizing the economy that could go beyond both the corporate-driven market and the commandist state. This new technology enabled them to make the most of the advantages of the distributed initiative that had been promised and not delivered by the market, while at the same time taking account of society's mutual needs – in theory, the responsibility of the state.

There is, indeed, a direct historical continuity with the rebellions of the 1960s. The use of the internet and associated technologies as tools to fulfil a dream of harmonious living (with each other and with the environment) has roots, interestingly, in the Californian counter-culture of the late 1960s. The continuity is not so much with the ideologically committed New Left politics of that era as with the more diffuse desire to change the world found in the 'back to the land' commune movement known as the 'new communalism'. This was characterized by a holistic vision of personal and social development, and commitment to an ethic of sharing and spreading information and innovation – epitomized and propagated by the *Whole Earth Catalog* associated with the supreme counter-cultural networker and entrepreneur Stewart Brand.[12]

Although some of the specific technologies go back to collaboration among technologists working on defence, the actual development of the internet was made possible by the miniaturization of computers that enabled individual users to have complete control over their machines. At the same time, the *Whole Earth Catalog* and the cultural logic of the new communalism provided the computer scientists – most of whom emerged out of the intellectual and organizational legacy of Cold War research – with the uses, and therefore marketing frames, for the new personal machines. Stewart Brand worked hard to bring these two groups together.

The open, sharing ethic underlying the use of these new tools was immeasurably strengthened by the creation of the World Wide Web by Tim Berners-Lee and his colleagues at the Conseil Européen pour la Recherche Nucléaire (CERN). He was quite explicit about its importance as an open resource for a changing society. This ethic of openness and change came into its own especially after the dot.com boom and the attempt to turn the new technologies towards a new capitalist expansion. For the generation coming to political consciousness when globalization – and, with it, the unleashing of the predatory lust of private corporations – was at its peak, the defence and development of the newly created 'digital commons' was a high priority among the many fronts of resistance to corporate-driven globalization.

An impressive feature of the 'free culture' movement, as the broad movement around an open internet became known, is that it developed open software and an open digital practice. Cities were usually hubs of this activity – some more than others. Barcelona was a strong centre of the alter-globalization movement and, not surprisingly, a hub for hackers and other free culture activists. The free software and digital commons networks were among those who got behind Barcelona en Comú, the alliance that secured victory for Ada Colau, leader of the movement against evictions (the Plataforma de Afectados por la Hipoteca (PAH) – in English, 'Platform for People Affected by Mortgages' – which defended those evicted by the banks for failing to pay their mortgages), in the 2015 mayoral elections, and, in coalition with other left-of-centre parties, won a majority on the council.

Barcelona en Comú has demonstrated strong support for a co-operative commons economy. It created Barcola, the node supporting and mapping the city's digital commons economy in collaboration with the municipal council. Barcola's co-ordinator, Mayo Fuster Morell, an internationally leading participator in and researcher on the digital commons and commons peer-to-peer production, clarifies the framework of its work with a useful definition of the digital commons:

> Information and knowledge resources that are collectively created and owned or shared between or among a community and that tend to be non-exclusive, that is, be (generally freely) available to third parties. Thus, they are oriented to favour use and reuse, rather than to exchange as a commodity. Additionally, the community of people building them can intervene in the governing of their interaction processes and of their shared resources.[13]

She goes on to give a good example of how a digital commons is often organized to meet needs that the market and state are incapable of meeting. Guifi.net, in Catalonia, is a free, open and neutral, mostly wireless, telecommunications community network, with over 27,000 active nodes and about 36,400 km of wireless links. It was created in a mountainous area for which there was no state or commercial Wi-Fi provision. So local communities worked to provide internet access by constructing a commons-based telecommunications network, first through collaboration with Wi-Fi companies, and, since 2009, also with fibre optics. Eventually guifi. net built up a reputation, receiving several awards, including one from the Generalitat of Catalonia in 2007 for providing internet access to rural areas, and one in 2015 for the Best Project in the category of Innovative Models, Business and Finance, awarded by the European Commission for developing an alternative sustainable and collaborative model around the commons.

Open plus co-operative: a force to be reckoned with

A notable development stimulated by the various movements around the digital commons and open software is a growing convergence with the more creative and imaginative parts of the co-operative movement. They have many shared values – transparency, open participation, distributed but social forms of ownership – and are beginning to discover each other. Both are significant economic players in their own right, and together comprise a serious alternative to conventional private profit-oriented capitalist businesses.

The idea of 'platform co-operatives' has been especially important as the basis of an alternative to platform capitalism – Uber, Airbnb, Deliveroo – because it focuses attention on the ownership of the digital platform and at the same time provides a means to increase the scale and reach of individual co-operatives.[14] Several such platform co-operatives have developed in Barcelona, with the encouragement of the municipal council, to provide renewable energy, shared transport and accommodation.

A wider-reaching example is Fairmondo, a global online market place owned by its local users – individual co-operatives. It is, effectively, a co-operative alternative to Amazon, illustrating the potential that early internet activists saw in the new networking tools for new forms of co-ordination and information-sharing beyond the capitalist market. Fairmondo is organized through a network of autonomous local co-operatives in each country that joins the platform.

It operates on the principle of democratic ownership open to everyone affected by the business. The cost of joining a co-operative must be affordable in terms of local purchasing power. Each member has one vote. The network is guided by principles of transparency and fair terms of collaboration with external and internal stakeholders (partners, staff, etc.), with low salary differentials. It is independent of individual vested interests, prohibiting large financial investments by individuals or non-co-operative organizations. If dividends are paid, broad participation and avoidance of distribution of large amounts to individuals must be ensured. At least 25 per cent of such surplus must be contributed to the common fund for further development of the project. There is a binding commitment to a democratic organizational culture: at least half of the co-operative's executive board must be elected by the employees.

Finally, Fairmondo is committed to open source and open innovation. In particular, it requires that the code of any platform must be made available under a licence that ensures publication of any further developments of that code are under the same terms. The experience of Fairmondo illustrates another distinctive feature of the social nature of the economic system when the new ICT tools are used for ethical and democratic ends. This is the blurring of the lines between producers and consumers and the promotion of responsible consumption, through the involvement of consumers and a degree of collaboration between producers and consumers in decisions about products and prices.

An increasingly important issue in the overlapping circles of digital commons, open software and co-operative networks is the development of a positive policy framework by exploring what role government can play to support them – especially given the predatory character of private corporations. In the face of this threat, Mayo Fuster Morell comments: 'I think we need to gain political control over political institutions in order to create public-commons alliances to confront the commons enclosure. A weak private–public alliance has resulted in the kidnap of political institutions; together they are creating what I call (borrowing from feminist theory) the "glass ceiling", working to ensure that the greater capacity for the commons to expand and gain centrality in the digital era is kept under control, and that commons are enclosed for profit purposes.'[15]

Barcelona en Comú is notably explicit about creating a new relationship between democratic forms of production and a participatory politics, but all these initiatives described in this chapter share a recognition that the old social democratic contract – leaving production to the private sector and concentrating exclusively on distribution – has broken down. A new politics requires a new economics that is concerned with production and ownership. These experiences indicate how changes in production, including in the organization of public administration, are already under way. New kinds of political action are needed on a civic–public alliance basis, to *enable* these changes to be fully realized. First, however, we need to explore how it might be possible to disseminate and spread a commons approach to shared resources, a co-operative and democratized form of production, and decentralized, participatory forms of public administration.

3

From Cells to Transitions

What then would a new politics from the left look like on a wider scale?

Experience has shown us, most recently in Greece, that achieving government power cannot be the overriding goal in an effective transition from a political economy driven by the imperatives of capital accumulation to one based on enabling each person to flourish for the benefit of all. I call this socialism, but as a vision with wide human appeal it has been shaped by many intellectual traditions and worked towards in practice by many different associations of labour – agricultural and landless, domestic and industrial – and many more of those struggling together and in creative collaborations, to pursue useful, dignified and pleasurable lives of mutual satisfaction and creative fulfilment.[1] A transition to such a society requires a process of self-organization at many different levels of the economy, as well as preparation for both the transformation of the internal power relations of the state and its relationships with different social classes and organizations. System change does not happen overnight, but is a complex process of transition in which gaining political office is only one specific and important moment.

A new politics from the left has 'power as transformative capacity' (see chapter 1) at its foundation – in its engine room, as it were. However, government power ('power as domination') is a necessary condition for realizing this capacity to the full, through the redistribution of wealth through taxation, the provision of public goods for all, and ensuring protection (of workers' rights, and of citizens' rights more generally, against the predatory and exclusionary/enclosing dynamics of the monopolistic capitalistic market) – and, potentially, government is one of several levels of co-ordination and participatory planning, and providing a transparent, democratically managed platform.

The emergence of economic alternatives beyond, in and against the state

Power as transformative capacity is generally, but not exclusively, located autonomously from the state and the market, but interfaces with both state and market in ways that are in constant flux. Examples of power as transformative capacity, like those in chapter 2, are not just ideas or demands, but alternatives realized or illustrated in practice. And as great social movements have grown up in recent decades contesting global corporate power in almost every sphere of life – from birth control, through education, food, water, transport, waste, wages, trade, technology and the future of the planet – the economy has become a sphere of civil action understood as a more or less autonomous productive force imbued with values and ideas and animated by its own organizations, networks and individuals.

Indeed, to understand the wider implications of this kind of power, we need to move away from the conventional, static distinctions between the market, the state and civil society, or the so-called 'third sector'. Instead (and here I draw heavily on the arguments of Robin Murray, perhaps the pre-eminent civil servant – as practitioner and analyst – of the civil economy[2]), we need to understand the key divide as between those parts of the economy that are driven by social goals (the social economy) and those subject to the imperatives of capital accumulation.

A New Politics from the Left

The economy driven by social goals is a hybrid of several sub-economies, all distinct in how they are financed, who has access to them and on what terms, what kinds of social relations are involved, how any surplus is distributed, and what kind of economic discipline is exerted to achieve these goals. They consist of the household, governed by relations of reciprocity; the state, funded by taxes and governed in theory by democratically determined social goals; and the section of the market that involves the exchange of equivalents – those few areas of the market (between small social or co-operative businesses) not yet dominated by capitalist enterprises and the private, profit-driven market.

In our present predominantly capitalist economy, they are all in different ways in conflict and in tension with economic forces driven by profit and capital accumulation, and are all vulnerable to being dominated by its imperatives. So the household can be a site of passive consumption and isolated childcare and housework, but can also be a place of mutual support and a sphere of social movements – both of feminism and of struggles for community control over services and land. Similarly, the state can be the willing handmaiden of global corporate markets, but its powers can also be used, where the balance of political power is favourable, to pursue social goals. There is nothing intrinsic to the state or household economies that drives them towards capital accumulation. Such economies are oriented to their own social goals; each can operate in some relation to a market – in Murray's words – 'in pursuit of their goals, without being drawn into the vortex of accumulation'.

How different civil economic initiatives pursue their social goals and in what relation to other institutions of the social economy, especially of the state, are vital questions. How left-oriented governments can strengthen and spread these initiatives as they follow their social goals is the central strategic issue. To use a biological metaphor, one could argue that the structure of the organism, the collaborative unit of the civil economy – the exercise of transformative capacity – is the essential foundation. The flourishing of healthy organisms in new forms of production – and, with it, a new politics – and their capacity to spread, is the key to the process of systemic transition. And the strength of these organisms must be a priority for an elected left-wing government or municipal council.

A New Politics from the Left

From creative initiatives to systemic transitions

Reflecting for a moment on the fate of the instances of power as transformative capacity described in chapter 2, one was never fully realized (the Lucas Aerospace alternative plan for socially useful production), another was isolated in too hostile an environment to spread (the Newcastle Unison experience of democratizing public administration), and one is multiplying impressively, partly with the support of a left alliance elected to municipal office (commons peer-to-peer production, especially the experience in Barcelona). These instances indicate that what matters for systemic transition is not only the health of the organism – the coherence, integrity and DNA of its transformative capacity – but also how favourable the environment is, especially the nature of government, or power as domination. An indication of the relevance of the thwarted initiatives is that their memory not only lives on but is being investigated and replicated in new forms.

The future of a new left politics will depend on the extent to which the past decade or so has seen not simply the occasional exceptional initiative of a transformative kind but also the emergence of clusters of organisms out of resistance to the dominant direction in which the imperative of capital is driving the economy, and, with it, society and human lives. They are, in effect, a practical expression of a belief that there are alternatives.

Several trends are especially notable: in particular, opposition to the socially destructive impact of global markets; challenges to the values and design of the technologies now destroying the foundations of human and animal life; the pervasive impact and potential of the new information and communication technologies, and the centrality of how they are controlled and by whom.

First, let us consider the various forms of counter-movement to corporate, global marketization and the social destruction it wreaks. Here we can observe movements of those whose land, livelihood and labour have been most directly and damagingly exploited in the aggressive drive to accumulate ('accumulation through dispossession', as David Harvey has understood it[3]): most noteworthy perhaps is La Via Campesina (LVC), founded in 1993 in Monds, Belgium, by farmers' organizations from Europe, Africa, Asia and Latin America, and by 2012 representing 500 million peasant farmers and their families, sharing a platform that insists: 'We do not own nature – it is not a commodity.' LVC campaigns for domestic food sovereignty and against the unequal and unregulated power of global markets, as a means of protecting peasant economic life based on reciprocity and rural ecology.

In countries especially hit by crisis, a number of civic economic initiatives are evident, from the development of local currencies to the take-over of abandoned industrial plants by worker co-operatives. In general, the number of co-operatives has been growing since the turn of the century, with a worldwide turnover of $3 trillion, and in several countries, North and South, over 20 per cent of the population belongs to a co-operative. Credit unions, a specific type of financial co-operative, rose from 37,000 in 2000 to 53,000 in 2010, their membership growing to 188 million and their total savings more than doubling to $1.2 trillion. What runs through all these initiatives is a strong sense of self-reliance and of self-consciously seeing themselves as struggling for a humane and ecological alternative to neoliberalism, an integration of the political and the economic.

Alternatives to core technologies

The same fusion of the political and the economic applies to a second kind of alternative to neoliberalism coming from the civil economy, which echoes and sometimes refers back to the Lucas Aerospace workers' alternative plan. I'm thinking here of responses to problems – of which climate change is the prime example – for which neither the market, nor the state as we know it, is providing answers. Such initiatives include a growing number and range of co-operatives and social enterprises (including municipal enterprises) which are – with some support from sympathetic governments, e.g. in the UK under Labour municipalities, and recently in Germany – addressing climate change by producing solar power, wind power and other kinds of renewable energies; the growth of community recycling networks; the creation of laboratories that show how products could be made without the use of hazardous chemicals; and a few cases of social-economy manufacturers of such products, including Vio-Me, the recuperated, worker-controlled factory in Greece. Social companies have built zero-energy housing. In Brazil, there have been remarkable social innovations in low-powered rural electrification. Like the Lucas Aerospace workers' plan, these responses are not about national models of economic planning, or a return to a version of Fabian planning 1945-style. Rather, they involve challenging the very models and values of production today and the consumption and technological choices and designs which dominate our economies and exacerbate damaging climate change.

There are similarly many examples of creative and collaborative value-driven civic solutions in response to other problems of contemporary capitalism: disease – especially lifestyle-related conditions like diabetes and obesity, and diseases related to mass agro-industry and food production – problems inadequately met by existing public provision and for which privatization is proving, at worst, disastrous, and at 'best', unreliable; maternity and childcare; and also care for the escalating numbers of the elderly. Those directly affected, or with skills and a vision of how much better such provision could be, are creating growing networks of alternatives and putting them into practice, often supported by public provision but improving on it. Similarly, in recreational spheres such as sport and entertainment, associations whose goals are social and cultural, rather than profit maximization, are experimenting with democratically controlled alternatives to profit-driven media, sporting and entertainment monopolies. Examples range from the growing number of community cable channels, and local and counter-cultural newspapers and websites, to football fans starting their own clubs or taking over ones facing problems. Real Madrid, Barcelona and Benefica are all co-operatives.

The favourable conditions created by new means of communication and of information exchange

Are there positive aspects of the contradictory character of contemporary capitalism that favour and explain the significant growth of civil, decentralized and socially driven productivity? Here we must take full account of the revolution in our means of communication and how, as well as enabling us to know more about what other people are doing and going through (we could see what was happening in Greece day by day, at Grenfell Tower hour by hour), it enables complex distributed initiatives to connect and become part of a system; it enables people to collaborate, across production and consumption, and to create platforms for co-operation and the infrastructure for a massive increase in the civil economy.

One especially notable counter-movement to the injustices of neoliberalism has been the continuing rise of 'fair trade'. This too, in combining ambitious circuits, flows and relationships between diverse micro-initiatives, has been significantly facilitated by the new tools of communication and sharing of information – carefully selected techno tools that can be controlled by their users not the ICT corporations. The term 'fair trade' was first used in 1988 to refer to the surge of new solidarity trading networks. It now takes many different forms, reflecting different stories of struggle and 'people to people' creativity in finding solutions – for example a Costa Rican co-operative producing bananas after Chiquita closed its plantations, and spaghetti produced by a co-operative of people with learning difficulties on land confiscated from the Mafia in Sicily. What they share is the attempt to socialize the market and remake the relationships, rules and purposes of international trade. Fair trade works at several different levels that can be in tension, although tension as such is not necessarily a problem – indeed, it can be highly productive. At one level, we've seen the various kinds of fair-trade shops, such as those of Altermercato in Italy (www. altermercato.it), which has 300 'world' shops with a turnover of $48 million. These Altermercato shops embody the global political economy in their products and provide information about campaigning on issues of labour conditions and the destructive environmental consequences of the commercial market. At another level, brands have been established, like Cafédirect (www.cafedirect.co.uk), between producer co-operatives, Twin Trading and other trading networks. It was sold in mainstream super-markets and coffee shops and, by 2005, had become the sixth-largest coffee brand in the UK. It used the profits made to provide an extensive programme of technical support for the producers. This model aimed to reverse the flow of power in the supply chain back to the producers and consumers and away from the private corporations. Twin extended the model to cocoa through Divine chocolate (www.divinechocolate.com), to fresh fruit (Agrofair UK) and to nuts (www.chooseliberation.com) – all of them, including Twin itself, co-owned by the producers. The next level was to form an interna-tional body, the Fairtrade Labelling Organization, which controls an international fair-trade mark and ensures consistency.[4]

The self-governance of these initiatives in the civil economy varies. Where the activity concerns pro-duction or distribution through the market, the most frequent form is the co-operative – an autonomous association of people united voluntarily to meet their common economic, social and cultural needs and aspirations through a jointly owned and demo-cratically controlled enterprise – with its emphasis on collaboration between those whose labour is making the activity possible for a shared goal.

There are many different kinds of co-operatives: worker co-operatives, consumer co-operatives, housing co-operatives, financial co-operatives and multi-stakeholder community co-ops. What they share is a common concern with collaboration on an egalitarian and democratic basis for a common purpose. Shared values, principles and mutual trust normally form the oil that makes them work, and hence these agreed principles are fundamental, and education about them is a high priority in the co-operative movement.

Another – and increasingly frequent – form to be found in the civil economy is that of 'the commons'. It has become an increasingly wide-spread self-description used mainly by those resisting privatization to highlight their rejection of the enclosing, commodifying pressures of the capitalist market, and their experience of the inadequacy of the state. The 'commons' also asserts the shared nature of the resource at stake and hence the need for governance to take the form of mutual responsibility and contribution. As a framework for managing shared natural resources, it gained mainstream attention when Elinor Ostrom won the Nobel Prize for Economics for her work on the sustainability of the commons. Activists in the open software, open culture movement have since appropriated the concept and applied it very fruitfully to what they describe as 'the digital commons' and/or 'the knowledge commons', so that it has become an inspiring rallying cry for protecting and extending the new knowledge commons of the twenty-first century, against the predatory corporate adventurers who see in the latest technologies a new El Dorado, which they rush to enclose and to mine for digital gold. Drawing on the work of others, I define the commons as a shared resource, which is co-owned or co-governed by a community of users and stakeholders, under the rules and norms of that community. There is no commons without active co-production (commoning), and without an important measure of self-governance. Thus, it differs from both public and state- or city-owned goods, and from private property managed by its owners.

Co-operatives and commons share a commitment to social goals and democratic processes and provide an actual working alternative to corporate control. Several municipalities have made support for collaboration between these and other parts of the social economy – small social businesses, for example, or informal associations of neighbours meeting shared needs – a way to gain democratic control over their local economies in the aftermath of the financial crisis of 2008, and to overcome their vulnerability to corporate power. Barcelona, for example, under the leadership of the radical, mainly civil movement, alliance Barcelona en Comú, has made support for a co-operative commons economy platform an important part of its economic strategy. We saw some of their initiatives in chapter 2. Such a platform was already autonomously beginning to form, and to make international links, and the approach of Barcelona en Comú, itself based on a convergence of civil initiatives, has a methodology of supporting autonomous initiatives rather than implementing its strategy in a centralized manner, under its own control. Since many of its activists have come from civil initiatives, rather than parties or political/administrative careers, they understand power as transformative capacity, from experience. It is in their political bones.

It is not only at a local level that political bodies are building alliances with co-operatives and commons initiatives. The United Nations Research Institute for Social Development (UNRISD) is working to bring together a very large alliance of social and solidarity initiatives with interested public bodies, in order to spread a social economy approach that will also share power with the poor and support their autonomous organizations. There is already some experience of national governments in Latin America supporting what is often termed 'the solidarity economy', meaning civil initiatives for a social economy but with a strong agenda of social and political change. In Brazil, for example, the government of Luiz Inácio Lula da Silva created a whole department for the solidarity economy. Sadly, it was soon marginalized as his government adopted a conventional corporate-led development strategy, aimed at opening up Brazil to the corporate global market.

Overcoming the labour movement's traditional divide of politics from economics

Governments today tend to support the global market (actively or passively). Labour movements have tended to leave politics to the political parties with which they are associated and to treat economics as a separate sphere. But if labour and co-operative movements used their power effectively, they could get governments, local as well as national, to support the economic alternatives being created by organized labour. There are a plethora of experiences here from which to learn, in a constructively critical manner. Movements and municipalities in the global South, from planning and literacy campaigns in Kerala to participatory budgets in Brazil, have pioneered a sharing of power with civil society in shaping public policy.

A growing number of experiences in the North, paralleling the growth of the civil economy, have involved radical left politicians who, witnessing the limits of strategies that relied exclusively on the state, began to use their elected positions to open and share state resources with transformative allies organizing economic alternatives. For example, paralleling the growth of the co-operative sector has been the development, across the world, of new institutions for supporting, protecting and disseminating co-operatives.

The experience of the relationship between co-operatives – as a significant example of the civil economy – and politics is especially revealing because it is such a long history, going back in some countries to the mid nineteenth century and the origins of the labour movement and socialism itself – indeed, the institutional divide between economics and politics had been transplanted from bourgeois society to the labour movement.

This is not a history that can even be summarized in a small book such as this, but we should note its beginnings and the contemporary state of play.[5] In the UK, co-operativism had its roots in the Owenite movement in the late 1820s, which believed in and practised the idea of co-operatives as the most coherent form of working-class self-organization and self-government. For Owenite co-operatives, association for the purpose of production was the beginning of politics. According to the pre-eminent social historian of the co-operative movement, Stephen Yeo, associational forms were being developed 'to create as well as to propose; to exchange as well as to produce; and deal with the future of working people as well as the products necessary for everyday life'. Government, in a sense, flowed from co-operative/associated production. As Yeo puts it: 'Government meant what *we* can do among ourselves, co-operatively and mutually, as much as it means what *they* – the government – must be asked to do' (original emphasis). Viewing them at their most radical and transformative, co-operative societies, according to Yeo, 'saw themselves as entities capable of reforming a complete new/old *social* order, using the word "social" in a stronger sense than is common today' (original emphasis). And he continues: 'They were oppositional in stance and hegemonic in ambition rather than safely alternative or subordinate.'

In 2013, however, when Cilla Ross from the Co-operative College conducted a survey of the political support which different governments gave to co-operatives, she found several examples where governments gave financial support and co-operatives took it on a strictly instrumental, 'value-free' basis. The values and principles of co-operatives were no longer the basis of a shared goal of transformation. She reports on co-ops in parts of the USA addressing social problems and creating dignified, if low-paid, jobs in areas abandoned by private capital. She describes how, on the other hand, state governments without the power to generate jobs on a large scale were needing immediate solutions. They gave financial support to co-ops. It was a pragmatic alliance. This is one direction in which the relation between co-operatives and politics has developed. In a sense, the divide continues: in response to social need, co-ops provide an elastoplast economy. Government provides them with a small amount of the revenue it gains from taxing those who have benefited from the de-industrialization of the areas in need.

But the survey also highlights countries where there are relationships between co-operatives and political authorities in which both share transformational goals and collaborate to advance the co-operative ideal. The process, as well as the shared values, is important to the integration of politics and economics. This is well illustrated by the recent experience of the French Canadian province of Quebec. There, when the Parti Québécois was in government, until 2013, it often – but not always – shared resources and combined different sources of knowledge in giving support to the relatively strong co-operative movement, whose origins were rural but which, since the end of the Second World War, had become a large, though somewhat bureacratized, national movement, organized through the Conseil québécois de la coopération et de la mutualité (CQCM). Here, the co-operative movement still bears some resemblance to its radical English forebears. Its members see themselves as laying foundations for, and, at the same time, showing the way towards, self-government. They have a confidence in the capacity of the social economy to produce the economic basis of a new order, and, through their numerous networks, they attempt to create a comprehensive basis for the self-government of everyday life. The radical dimension of the co-operative movement has been especially taken forward by the younger Chantier de l'économie sociale (a network of networks in the social economy). This group worked together with the CQCM, the network of worker co-operatives, and the government's special ministry for supporting co-operatives to co-write a legal framework for the social economy. According to those involved, it marks a significant and unique step forward in gaining legitimacy and recognition for this economy. Support from the regional government has been a resource, a protection, and a source of legitimacy and economic sustainability (through government procurement, for example, the place of co-operatives in the Quebec regional economy is guaranteed). And the co-operative movement, in turn, enables Quebec's governments to address problems of inequality and social cohesion. The government's co-operative ministry has also prioritized citizen education and capacity-building in co-operative self-government. Quebec could be said, as a result, to have the basis of an ecology of different forms of social ownership, and with it an ecology of different kinds of knowledge. Under the recent Liberal government, however, which defeated the self-defined 'progressive nationalist' Parti Québécois, all this has been made precarious by a progamme of extreme austerity measures.

The experience of the 1980s Greater London Council, under the political leadership of Ken Livingstone, also illustrates institutions developed, on the basis of shared transformational values, to support, protect and develop the capacity of civil initiatives which, at least when the Livingstone-led Labour group was first elected, were quite strong and self-confident, though beginning to face the onslaught of Thatcher's destruction of anything assertive of society – 'There is no such thing as society' becoming, in her hands, a self-fulfilling prophecy. Abolished by the Thatcher government in 1986, this radical municipal regime never had the time that successive Québécois governments have had to develop what I would call 'new ecologies of social ownership and of plural knowledge'. It made important steps in this direction, but such complex and organic relationships require time to take root and mature, as I discuss below.

The nature of the GLC as a municipal rather than national authority (so without the military dimension of national state power) and as a municipal power of a strategic kind – rather than delivering everyday services as a town council does – meant that the elected politicians had to carry out their radical manifesto with very clearly limited powers. It was particularly evident that, if they were to honour their manifesto promises, they depended on strong and creative alliances with the organizations and communities of Londoners. The aim of GLC councillors was not simply to manage the municipal state in a traditionally paternalistic way to meet what they believed to be the needs of the people. Rather, they knew they must transform the state, so that it was both more open to, and supportive of, the creative capacities and associational power of the civil economy, and more intransigent in resisting the imperatives of private capital. This dependence on alliances with the people of London grew as the GLC came increasingly into conflict with Thatcher's government on the other side of the Thames.

Two principles with wider relevance were important in this alliance with mostly self-organized citizens. First, there was the concept of 'productive democracy': the idea of the state and the civil economy, especially through the organized capacities of labour – household and precarious labour, as well as waged – as productive, hence breaking the dependence of democratic politics on private capital. Second was the vital role of the state in supporting – not substituting for – the realization and development of the capacities of civil economic associations.

This active support took many forms. Sometimes it was a matter of using the GLC's powers over land to block financial speculators, for example in supporting the community development plans of the people of Coin Street, Waterloo – a prime site by the

Thames – against City office developers; sometimes, it used its responsibilities for 'the interests of all or some of the people of London',[6] plus its high public profile, to support workers organizing across multinationals such as Ford and Kodak, enhancing their industrial action with public inquiries to expose and question the companies' sacrifice of jobs and communities to the incessant search for profit.

Sometimes it supported civil organizations in producing positive plans for socially useful jobs, whether by negotiating, and paying for, time off and research support for workplace shop stewards to develop alternative plans for run-down industries, such as furniture production, or by working with women's groups across London on proposals for childcare that the GLC would then fund. The aim was always to reintegrate the state and civil society to realize the creative capacities of labour in the interests of all.

Beyond the competitive drive for profit

We are still in an early phase of a transition from an economic system driven by the competitive imperative for profit and capital accumulation to economic relations driven by social values and the creativity of those people discarded by the imperatives of private profit. The former system – capitalism – has in recent years lost its equilibrium and legitimacy as inequality has skyrocketed and financial flows have taken off into a world of their own, casting aside any regard for the real economy of human lives, capacities and needs.

The systemic character of this transition is likely to be historically and geographically specific, though with many shared logics and practices arising from being socially and environmentally driven, and democratic in its processes.

What concept best encapsulates the hybrid combinations of ownership and knowledge by which this transition is being worked on daily, with and without state support? I would suggest that the idea of *ecologies of ownership* and *ecologies of knowledge* captures the wider potential of attempts to overcome the debilitating division between economics and politics. The metaphor of *ecologies* would seem appropriate to the organic, unpredictable nature of the transition. First, the concept of 'ecologies' emphasizes the dependence of any economy and polity on the natural environment. Second, it conveys the idea of a complex, plural, interdependent system with many levels and relationships, which is, simultaneously, organic rather than machine-like, and whose relationships change and develop in relation to each other and to the natural environment (which underpins and is a condition of the system's reproduction). This understanding of human relationships also makes assumptions about human agency quite contrary to those of orthodox economics. The conventional model of the economy as a 'complex machine' reduces human agency to a variable whose behaviour as part of the machine can be predicted on the basis of mathematical equations that assume the rational individual actor. My understanding of agency involves a much less predictable, richer and – I believe – more realistic notion of human motivation and rationality, one which takes account of how reason is closely combined with emotion, intuition, personal history and experience – and probably much more. It also understands individual human beings as social beings – whose basic tools of existence, language and knowledge, are the product of social relationships.

The machine model of the economy also underpins and reinforces the division between politics and economics: politics is an 'intervention' in the economic machine. The idea was that the state 'intervened' in society like an engineer fixes a machine. The role of the labour movement, the mass of party supporters, whether party activists or union members, was to get the engineers in place to deploy the instruments of state. Implementation of policy was understood as an entirely technical matter, best left to the experts. The way, for example, in which the nationalized industries were to be administered was not seen as complex or a political matter. It could be left to the technocrats, civil servants or academic experts, or captains of industry (as industrial experts) brought in for the purpose.[7]

The civil economy is commonly regarded as the economy of the marginal: interesting and worthy but with little power to influence the mainstream. In fact, however, today's civil economy is the result of powerful social movements on the great issues of today: food and agriculture, international finance and trade, consumption, waste, land and the environment, water, and the media. These movements have on several occasions blocked the machine. They have sought to reverse it too, and, when this has failed, they have taken action themselves both collectively and in their everyday lives: they have occupied factories and restarted production on the basis of different values – human- and environment-centred rather than profit-driven; fostered different, egalitarian and collaborative relationships – with themselves as workers and with communities around the factory; experimented with alternative currencies, fair trade, and socially useful production, as we have seen in this chapter; and, increasingly, elected politicians who treat the economy not as a machine to be fine-tuned but as a variety of human relationships to be engaged with. Moreover, in order to enable these relationships to flourish without being destroyed by the profit-driven machine, they can act to expand the ecologies of ownership and knowledge. They can use powers of government to take resources that had been servicing the private capitalist economy and make them public. (Turning money into a public system and the banks into public utilities would be a good example here, a proposal clearly elaborated by Mary Mellor.[8])

As far as knowledge is concerned, governments can have access to information (one necessary element of a sustainable ecology of knowledge) giving an overview of the economy. Traditionally, what is known, and how it used, is the exclusive property of government and its corporate allies. But experience has shown how it can be used as a resource for co-ordinating an economy based on popular democracy. An interesting experience was the cybernetic system used in Chile under Salvador Allende before his government was destroyed by the USA in 1973, which, instead of being a means of centralized planning, was a resource for the network of worker-controlled enterprises throughout the Chilean economy.[9]

These complex ecologies thus depend on the people who are part of them and can probably only be sustainable with a flexible system of participation, so that citizens can find the rhythms of active engagement that suit them – not requiring everyone to go to every meeting and keep up the same levels all the time, and using good information and communication systems, including small informal gatherings, all enabling people to keep informed and make inputs in different ways.

The problem is: through what kind of political strategies can we create the conditions in which these ecologies of social ownership, open and plural knowledge and flexible participation would predominate?

4

Conclusions: On Questions of Political Strategy and Organization

Let us return to the 'long revolution' and place recent events in Europe and in the UK in the context of what, as we have already seen, Raymond Williams, writing in 1961, described as 'the rising determination, almost everywhere, that people should govern themselves' – a lengthy, difficult and complex revolution that is nonetheless 'a genuine revolution', changing people and places, despite deeply ingrained resistance to change.

His idea of a 'genuine revolution' draws on his understandings of the material, everyday nature of culture, existing – often unrecognized – alongside more official forms of culture: 'The questions I ask about our culture are questions about our general and common purposes, yet also questions about deep personal meanings. Culture is ordinary, in every society and in every mind.'[1]

A New Politics from the Left

This idea of culture being 'ordinary' connects closely with my stress on understanding 'everyday knowledge' – tacit, practical knowledge – as a foundation for the possibilities of purposeful, but also experimental and always unfinished, collective political agency. Tacit knowledge is an important part of the everyday creation of meaning through conversation, collaboration and various other forms of communication – visual and oral memories, literary works, film, music, novels, painting and so on. The daily flow of the production of meanings and problem-solving knowledge, like the development of product designs or of new ways of organizing, is often the result of serendipity, intuition and hunch, and other forms of tacit knowledge, which are often difficult to codify in statistical or other centralizable forms. Such knowledge is, nevertheless, real. Moreover, in opposition to the theorists of the free market, far from being inherently individual, this practical knowledge is sharable and is a vital dimension of creative and also experimental collaboration.[2]

This practical form of knowledge and the popular capacity with which it is often associated are, for me, the foundation of a new politics from the left – foundations on which participatory economic democracy can bring together politics and economics in a new way, on the basis of cultural, as well as economic and social, equality.

The material importance of everyday knowledge and how it should combine with and draw on other kinds of knowledge, including expert knowledge of various kinds, was borne out in the man-made tragedy of the fire that ravaged the lives and homes of 124 families, 600 people, living in Grenfell Tower, a 24-floor tower block in North Kensington, part of the richest borough in the country: the Royal Borough of Kensington, home to several royal palaces. 'Man-made tragedy' because it need not have happened had councillors and officials listened to the concerns and practical knowledge of residents going back to at least 2013, when faulty wiring led to a terrifying power surge that caused an electricity black-out. Grenfell Tower was managed by an arm's-length company, which in turn contracted out the block's £10 million refurbishment to a chain of private companies, making the accountability of those responsible for the Tower's safety very indirect, to say the least.

Residents complained to the board and officials of the Kensington and Chelsea Tenant Management Organisation (KCTMO) about the lack of sprinklers, failure to provide an escape route or a central alarm, rubbish accumulated in the one narrow stairway, inadequate access for emergency services, and several other problems that they witnessed daily. They submitted reports on cladding, and drew attention to other expert opinions that reinforced their concerns. When their worries were dismissed by the KCTMO, they took them to the council, a Conservative council on which there were only eleven Labour councillors out of a total of fifty-one. They were again dismissed and, according to newly elected Labour MP Emma Coad Dent, 'frequent complainers' were blacklisted. In desperation, they wrote in November 2016: 'It is a terrifying thought but Grenfell Action Group firmly believe that only a catastrophic event will expose the ineptitude and incompetence of our landlord . . . Only an incident that results in a serious loss of life will allow the external scrutiny to occur that will shine a light on KCTMO and bring them to justice.'[3]

In a most horrific manner, this event, and the residents' actions and councillors' inactions, drove home Labour's message at the general election: that the country was being run by the few at the expense of the many, even to the point of robbing them of life. In the constituency of Kensington and Chelsea, the many had gained the confidence to rebel and overturn the 8,000-or-so majority of the latest generation of Conservative MPs, and had elected their first Labour MP. Four days later came the fire. In her maiden speech, Coad Dent set out the context of extreme poverty and inequality. In a borough where houses were valued in the millions and the Council had reserves of nearly £300 million, child poverty was at 25 per cent. Some Conservative councillors, she suspected, 'don't believe that social tenants have the right to live in desirable areas like Kensington', and would even say to her, in response to complaints about their housing, 'they should move away'.[4]

Here then, in the charred carcass of Grenfell Tower, looming over the lives of the extremely poor and the extremely wealthy, was a symbol of the hollowing-out of democracy through inequality, privatization and austerity, reinforced by the ruling elite's contempt for the poor. Here is a crisis of politics deepened by a crisis of knowledge: of whose knowledge matters – and even counts – as knowledge.

When Jeremy Corbyn, in his election slogan 'For the many, not the few', echoed the verse from Shelley's great tribute to the dead of Peterloo, the *Masque of Anarchy* – in which he called on the people to

> Rise like lions after slumber
> In unvanquishable number . . .
> Ye are many – they are few

– he was not treating 'the many' as simply numbers, voters, population statistics. Like Shelley, in his comparison with the dignified, intelligent and powerful lion – the king of beasts – he is treating 'the many' as knowing, dignified citizens, without a hint of the superiority that is so often in the demeanour of many MPs. Not surprisingly then, Jeremy Corbyn went to meet those who gathered in shock and in anger, as well as in grief, at the foot of Grenfell Tower the day after the fire, and listened and comforted and discussed what should be done to call the culprits to account. And these people welcomed him as a friend. They had refused to meet Theresa May, whose party treated them, and the safety and living conditions of their homes, with such disastrous contempt. A police escort was necessary to protect her as she left the area.

While Grenfell Tower is a negative example of the public value of practical knowledge, this book began with positive examples, created through productive civil initiatives in the spheres of manufacturing, local government services and information and communication. Both the action of the Grenfell Tower residents in gathering their shared information and concerns, and the initiatives described in chapter 2, contrast with the old politics of knowledge in its paternalist Fabian forms (which have had a formative and lasting influence on the institutions of the Labour Party) – that is, meeting social needs according to what the experts considered appropriate in the context of a social democracy in which economic and social equality is combined with the presumption of cultural superiority. They contrast too with the technocratic New Labour form of old politics, which dispensed with all forms of equality – economic, social and cultural – in deference to the imperatives of the private market.

After discussing this, I then sketched my vision of change as a transition driven by the exercise of power as transformative capacity, supported by a government sharing the same goals and willing to decentralize power at the same time as protecting civil initiatives from the destructive power of the private corporate-driven market. My approach was not to lay out a completed system design (an impossible task) but to point to trends and agents of change and to the overlapping ecologies – of social ownership and knowledge – and flexible, multi-level processes of participation – that would be a condition of an effective transition.

It follows from the hybrid combinations of power, knowledge and ownership suggested in chapter 3 that a key strategic question concerns alliances between different kinds of organizations, for common goals and on the basis of shared values. A good example would be in energy: here the implication of my argument would be the combination of local energy co-operatives and regional public energy companies based on renewable energy sources – in the framework of a cap on energy prices – with a publicly owned national grid. Elements of this combination – co-operatives and community networks generating electricity on the basis of renewables – might already be in existence, as they are in the UK and several other countries, but regional public companies and public ownership of the national grid either await a change of government, as in the UK, or, in a more decentralized country such as Germany, exist in only one or two regions.

This material change, taking place through transformative collective action rather than waiting for a change of government – and also contributing to such a political change through the propaganda of practice – could apply to many spheres where there is a need for different levels, civil and governmental, to converge. Indeed, a strategy based on the new politics, using the distinction between power as transformative capacity and power as domination, would be exactly to combine these two levels. In a sense, this extends Gramsci's war of manoeuvre into the sphere of production and the creation of working, prefigurative solutions in the here and now, as a preparation for winning government.

This process of creating what have been called 'prefigurative alternatives' occurred most notably in the 1970s and 1980s. We saw some examples in chapter 2, and then wider trends moving into the 1990s and the twenty-first century. They were blocked, and sometimes entirely defeated, as neoliberal governments gained office in many countries, or social democratic governments were compliant with the increasingly deregulated global capitalist market in the UK, Spain and Greece – to name but a few. In this context, powerful movements and networks began to feel they had hit the limits of autonomous self-organizing. The student and alter-globalization movements of Greece were among the first, forming, in 2006, the coalition of movements and small parties that became Syriza, which six years later gained 27 per cent of the vote, before, in January 2015, becoming the governing party. In Spain, the powerful '15 M' or *Indignado* movement, including solidarity networks such as the Mortgage Victims' Platform (Plataforma de Afectados por la Hipoteca, PAH), felt they had hit a glass ceiling when millions of signatures calling for abolition of Spain's cruel mortgage repossession laws were ignored, while corruption and clientelism were rife. In a story common to many Spanish cities – from Barcelona and Madrid to Coruña and Zaragoza – citizens started to wonder what would happen if the movement also tried to occupy the political institutions.[5] Different movements and groups produced a variety of organizations with electoral ambitions: Podemos nationally, and many city-wide alliances, including Barcelona en Comú. Then a Very British Breakthrough: the improbable rise of Jeremy Corbyn, followed by a relative electoral success that left the political pundits and many of his supporters gasping with surprise – and varying degrees of horror and delight.

My thinking on the new politics and its contrast with the old is shaped especially by experience and study of British politics, mainly in relation to the left of the Labour Party. The Lib Dem members of my family joke that I search the world for socialism, only to find it here at home! So – returning home, as it were – my focus in these conclusions is on Corbyn, Momentum and a new politics from the left in the UK, though I will draw on comparisons with Greece and Barcelona.

The most distinctive – and probably unique – feature of the Corbyn phenomenon is that this radical transformative left politics has emerged *within* a social democratic party, though driven significantly by long-marginalized – one might even say suffocated – movement energies *outside* (energies and activists that were attracted to Corbyn – himself a consistent activist and an emphatically *non-parliamentarist* MP – in spite of their hesitations about the Labour Party). My conclusions, while not trying to predict the likely scenarios for left politics in the UK, draw from the Corbyn experience and from that of Syriza in Greece, and of Barcelona en Comú in Spain, to argue for a radicalization of the relations between electoral politics and extra-parliamentary alternatives – based on understanding power as transformative capacity.

The energies of the movement that lifted Jeremy Corbyn to leadership came from environmental campaigners and direct-action groups, those with a memory of the thwarted but massive movement to stop the war in Iraq, radicalized by growing inequality, austerity and the 2008 financial crash, and by the mounting threat to the survival of the planetary ecological system – as well as from thousands of trade union members angered by government cuts and their consequences for public services, local government and the lives and prospects of young people. Jeremy Corbyn, as an activist in many different struggles, symbolized a new effort from below to open the party to becoming a movement for radical change, through his modesty and daily support for others in struggle. But a stubborn question remains: what about transforming the Labour Party? To do so, the Corbyn momentum (*sic*) will need to be sustained not just over one joyous summer but during a possible four-year wait until the next general election. Moreover, it will need to extend and deepen its support for a process of sustained transformation.

The deeply embedded nature of the mentalities of the old politics in the institutions of the Labour Party, with its assumptions about the incapacity of working people to develop positive solutions to the problems faced by them, their workmates and their families, makes changing these institutions very difficult, if not impossible. Indeed, following the analysis of Ralph Miliband, author of the classic work on the Labour Party *Parliamentary Socialism*,[6] I was not convinced that the party could be changed. In *Labour: A Tale of Two Parties*, I argued, in agreement with Miliband, that it could not.[7] I only joined after Corbyn became leader, though I had worked with the left of the party through many different movements and local forums, especially in Tyneside, Manchester and London.

Conclusions

I was not the only sceptic, nor the only sceptic who changed their mind. It is necessary, therefore, before exploring the meaning of a new politics on the left for Labour, to explore how Miliband's arguments now stand in the light of the rise of Corbyn and Momentum, the movement that consolidated his support.

First, the Labour Party remains fundamentally what Miliband described as a 'parliamentarist' party: more dogmatic about parliament than about socialism. In his analysis, the membership has no effective power to change this. He would not regard a relatively successful election campaign – such as Corbyn's – as proof of anything very radical; it's the one moment when the PLP appreciates (indeed, positively needs) all those radical, energetic members they normally despise. Richard Crossman (quoted by Miliband in support of his argument) famously described the role of the party's extra-parliamentary membership as follows: 'In order to maintain the enthusiasm of party militants to do the organising work for which the Conservative Party pays a vast army of workers, a constitution was created which apparently created full party democracy while excluding these members from effective power.'[8] How much has really changed in the five or so decades since Crossman wrote this?

Second, there is the moderating influence of the trade unions, especially their leadership. It was they who in the past – for example, against Tony Benn, after an initial show of support – ultimately provided the 'stabilizing' bulwark of the structural, lasting power of parliamentarism. True, currently there are key trade unions which support Corbyn, in response to the pressures of a membership radicalized by austerity, but how sustainable is this likely to be in the long term?

We need to engage with these kinds of questions because, to be strategically effective, we need to address, even at the highpoint of our enthusiasm and excitement, the problems we face in carrying through the logic of Corbyn's victories to transform the Labour Party itself.

Winning from the left

The appeal of Corbyn's straightforward, humane, calm and encouraging leadership, combined with John McDonnell's unrelenting opposition to austerity, has proved dramatic. It's been an appeal strengthened rather than weakened by Corbyn's ability to withstand the concerted attack of most of the PLP and media, including the *Guardian*, all showing a disregard of the actual views of Labour Party members. This, plus Momentum's social media organizing, facilitated a grassroots-driven general election campaign that produced the first example, beyond the extraordinary circumstances of the immediate post-war period, of Labour Party electoral success – though not yet victory – on the basis of an appeal from the left. (Even in 1945, it was not the leadership but the activists and voters who were on the left.) At the same time as turning the Tory tabloids into paper tigers and showing the liberal commentariat to be out of touch, this electoral success from the left removes one important sustaining shibboleth of centrist left parliamentarism: the insistence – an article of faith, really – that, because of the peculiarities of the British electoral and party system, Labour can only win elections by moving to the centre, to attract the 'floating voters in the marginals'. Accordingly, given the importance of unity against the Conservatives (under a first-past-the-post electoral system), the left in the party and the trade unions have always moderated their demands and subordinated themselves to the imperatives of unity and electoral success, on terms set by the PLP.[9] This has meant a prohibition on politicized industrial struggles, and on any questioning of the government's nuclear defence policy, or of the

British state in all its imperial and martial feigning of 'Greatness'. Corbyn, attacked by all the possible and most extreme demonizing taboos ever thrown at a party leader, broke this imprisoning cycle.

It is true that, in the 2017 election manifesto, Corbyn made compromises on defence, to be consistent with party policy as it is. In response to the Manchester terrorist attack, however, when campaigning resumed, Corbyn treated the electorate as adults and addressed not just the attack, which he, of course, condemned, but the causes of it. He pointed out that, after sixteen years of the disastrous 'War on Terror', Britain is still subject to terrorist attacks, which he connected to the failures of British foreign policy, among other causes. As Andrew Murray, a past chair of 'Stop the War'[10] who was seconded from Unite to join the inner core of Corbyn's election campaign team, commented: 'This was a courageous thing for him to do. It would have been far easier to simply condemn and leave it at that. But that would have not been levelling with the public. He said there has to be a serious debate, with everything on the table . . . that there is a connection between British foreign policy this century and the continuation of terror attacks in Britain. In so far as no party political leader has dared make this linkage publicly since 2001, we can say that a Rubicon has been crossed.' I would add that Corbyn's statement now opens the way for developing, with the party, an alternative to traditional notions of national defence, shaped, as they are, by entrenched mentalities of empire and a so-called 'special' Anglo-American relationship.

Thatcher's destruction of trade union corporatism

In Miliband's analysis, parliamentarism was reinforced by a corporate and sectional trade unionism concerned with bargaining over workplace issues, while delegating wider political issues of welfare, taxation and industrial, macroeconomic and foreign policy to the PLP. Here Miliband's concept of 'Labourism', complementary to 'parliamentarism', was of the Labour Party as an instrument for a sectoral, corporate interpretation of the interests of organized labour, reflecting 'the growing integration of the trade unions into the framework of modern capitalism'.[11]

Miliband understood that a sustained integration of the trade unions into capitalism was a condition of the Labour Party's power structure, ensuring that the union leaderships would accept the confines of parliamentarism and Labourism. This in turn requires stable corporatist relationships of political economy, whereby the trade unions are acquiescent and integrated at the factory, company and government level as 'partners', though effectively locked in permanent institutional subordination. After Thatcher's sustained attack on the trade unions, left virtually unaltered by New Labour governments, such conditions do not hold in the UK and this, together with other newer forms of 'popular insubordination', led to the breakdown of the alliance between the PLP and the trade union leadership at the apex of Labour's power structure. Corbyn's victory in the 2015 leadership election owed a lot to the pent-up anger of trade union members, not only in the long aftermath of Thatcherism but in response to New Labour's continuation of too many Thatcherite policies. Some trade union leaders, such as Len McCluskey, General Secretary of Unite, either shared this anger, or, as with Dave Prentis at UNISON, could not hold it back from determining their union's decision in both leadership elections.

Furthermore, under Ed Miliband's leadership, the centralizing grip that Blair and Mandelson had imposed as part of their obsession with control was somewhat loosened. A few left-wingers were chosen by their constituency parties and got through the net of nationally monitored parliamentary selection.

Moreover, the leadership election rules were changed so that individual trade union members (rather than the union block vote) and party supporters could vote for the leader. Contrary to the expectation of the Blairites who insisted on this – assuming that 'one person, one vote' would give what they believed to be a 'moderate' trade union membership a voice against 'unrepresentative' trade union leaders – it actually enabled members to voice their anger at the austerity regimes of both the Conservatives and subsequent New Labour governments, and it enabled other social movement activists, who after the experience of Blair would never have dreamt of joining the Labour Party, to pay a small 'supporter's fee' and vote in the leadership election.

As the economistic or syndicalist dynamics of militant trade unionism were blocked by anti-trade union laws, the pent-up anger of trade union and other activists found a new political expression then, through their support for Jeremy Corbyn. During the course of the 2015 leadership election campaign, almost 100,000 trade union members directly signed up to join the Labour Party, while even more became registered supporters. In such dynamic and volatile conditions, the reproduction of the formations of Labourism and parliamentarism could no longer be guaranteed.

A New Politics from the Left

Towards a transformative party?

Taken together, the collapse of the conventional assumption that Labour can only win by tacking to the right, and the radicalization of the active union membership as a result of the end of trade union integration into the economy, are important in ending the permanent domination of the right. But they don't yet indicate whether or not Labour can become a truly transformative left party. By this, I mean a party that would prepare for government and govern in a way that transformed the state, making it sufficiently strong to confront and oppose private capital, tax evaders and the City, and, at the same time, sufficiently decentralized and participatory to facilitate the transformative capacities of workplace and community organizations, and enhance the power of local authorities, in the way described in chapter 3.

A facilitative use of political office in practice

Theoretical arguments are best illustrated – and developed – in actual practice. A current attempt to govern in a way which supports the building of transformative capacity has been taking place for the last twenty months or so in Barcelona, where, in 2015, the citizen platform Barcelona en Comú was elected as the minority municipal government, with Ada Colau as mayor, and a wave of activists from social movements responsible for the government of their city. An important break from old forms of power – power as domination – has been an explicitly 'feminized politics'. 'You can be in politics without being a strong arrogant male, who's ultra-confident, who knows the answer to everything', explains Colau. She exemplifies an alternative political style that openly expresses doubts and contradictions. This is reinforced by a values-based politics that emphasizes the role of community and the common good, and prioritizes the policies designed to build on that vision.

But most important, and consistent with this feminization of politics, is a break from traditional notions whereby, if you hold public office, you somehow 'have power'. On the contrary, the view of Barcelona en Comú is that 'power is the capacity to bring about change' and 'the occupation of the institutions is only one part of what makes change possible'.[12] Barcelona en Comú was born out of decades of movements confronting the corruption of, and repression by, the political class, and challenging them with direct action that sought to provide solutions to people's needs in the present – for example, stopping evictions. The thinking behind the formation of the coalition was that, faced with the limits of mobilizing outside the institutions, they had instead to try to 'occupy the political institutions', as one specific dimension of the same movement that was taking over the squares.

The combination of power at the base with the tools of political office

Occupying the institutions brought its own complications and, most notably, its own compromises, in a context where Barcelona en Comú is leading the City Council through Ada Colau, but it only holds eleven out of its forty-one seats. These eleven representatives have proved effective and resilient in struggles within the confines of the Council, but the coalition is very clear that, as Reyes and Russell put it, 'The power to act comes from a combination of occupying both the institutions and the squares'[13] – a combination, in other words, of social movements organizing and exercising leverage, creating a social force that can be coupled with the particular institutional power that can be deployed by occupying positions in a municipal council.

Conclusions

This stress on *combining* the power of social movements – generally, power as transformative capacity – and the power of occupying/winning positions in the institutions – power as domination – is a common aspiration or claim of organizations that describe themselves as aiming to create a new politics.

But the dynamics of the two dimensions of what is often portrayed as a united movement tend to pull in opposite directions, caused by the pressures on the left inside the institutions becoming dominant. The result has been that the movements, usually seen as the secondary dimension – despite rhetoric to the contrary – have been subordinated to what has all too often become a decidedly old way of managing the political institutions.

Whether or not the Labour Party can be changed in this direction depends, I suggest, on two factors. One is whether the deep and continuing divisions evident in the PLP and the apparatus can be overcome – not to produce a bland consensus or a ruthlessly controlled machine *à la* Tony Blair, only this time behind Jeremy Corbyn, but to open up more creative debate to address real tensions in the nature of the transition. The second is whether Momentum and the radical party membership (new and old) can combine the arduous process of maintaining a dynamic of internal change in the party with engaging in transformative initiatives in the wider society.

On the first question, the nature of the divisions in the party, especially the PLP and the apparatus, is difficult to predict since the June 2017 general election, but it seems, from first impressions, that those previously hostile are likely to move in one of two directions. One section of the PLP, and some previously hostile members of the party apparatus who will always be impressed by the ability to win votes and who shared many of Corbyn's policy commitments, but just did not think he was electorally credible, will now, with the interests of the party to the fore, be supportive of his leadership into the next election. Another more sectarian grouping, including ideological Blairites, committed to the free market, opposed to public ownership and somewhat trapped in a residual Cold War mentality – whose ideal world would be run by Hillary Clinton, Emmanuel Macron and Tony Blair – will continue to organize covertly, but with added determination, to ensure that Corbyn will never be Prime Minister. The problem for them is that, in the past, they have always been the electorally successful part of the Labour Party, and therefore hegemonic within a party whose members and activists are united by a desire to defeat the Tories and form a government. This foundation of their predominance has been blown apart by the 2017 election – though they try to deny that the result had anything to do with a positive campaign by Corbyn.

The second question is whether Momentum and the radical membership can combine the internally oriented process of changing the Labour Party – a long and sometimes necessarily tedious march through the institutions – with the outward-reaching engagement with the kinds of social movements and productive civil initiatives already described, as well as the electioneering that combines an element of both. This was certainly the original intention of Momentum, but the pressures to focus inwardly have been immense, especially when Corbyn and his leadership have faced internal attack. Indeed, electioneering preparations for the next, decisive general election are already to the fore. It seems, however, that many Momentum activists – through a process of branches learning from one another, and with the support of a generally enabling, rather than controlling, HQ, and through skilled and varied use of the internet and a personal, genuinely friendly and open culture – have found a way of enabling members to engage in the campaigns and initiatives about which they are enthusiastic, while at the same time being fully informed about the moments when their support is needed to achieve a change in the local party. In this way, they have created a flexible and varied system of participation, according to activists' individual circumstances, capacities and preferences.

Corbyn's election successes – not forgetting that 14 million people voted for one of the most reactionary Tory governments in recent history – have given him and Momentum apparent hegemony in the party and greater legitimacy in wider society. Exactly how far the hegemony in the party can be stabilized and built on when the centre and right are clearly organizing behind the scenes to weaken Corbyn's hold is uncertain.[14] And how the success during the election in consolidating party unity on the basis of the 2017 manifesto will be followed through is unclear, but hopeful. What an electorally successful left party, aiming for a radical transformation of the capitalist state and of the economy, involves in practice is uncertain; but the negative lessons of Greece warn harshly against any separation from the radical social movements from which their support came, and on whose transformative power Corbyn and his team depend, to achieve the changes they have promised and for which they were elected.

Conclusions

By way of a strategic conclusion, then, I would suggest the debates in the Labour Party – and, indeed, the broader discussions and alliances on the left which will become increasingly important – can most productively be framed not by the traditional categories inherited from the Cold War, of left equalling more state and right equalling more market, but as between those who uphold the existing institutions of the British state, with its separation of parliamentary politics from the struggles and alternatives rooted in civil society, and those who are rooted in those struggles as the basis of a new productive, and participatory, politics. What is required – and, under Jeremy Corbyn's leadership, is possible – is a Labour Party that no longer is divided along these old lines (although, for some, these will remain), but more importantly works in permanent creative tension with refounded and renewed forms of representative and party democracy, in common cause with those who are pursuing the same ambitions directly, through exemplary changes in the here and now, predominantly outside parliament.

Participatory democracy is sometimes dismissed as somehow mindless, the politics of 'the mob'. One implication of my argument is that, on the contrary, it is a case of active minds linking their experience to that of others, and thinking through the sometimes conflicting implications of both, far more than in conventional forms of oligarchic government. It is a process involving a collective self-consciousness, of which one aspect must be self-discipline – including knowing when to stop talking. In that sense, participatory processes are microcosms of the process of decentralization essential to the new politics from the left, a daily organizing practice of letting go, sharing and no longer controlling. Shutting up is not always my strong point, but I think now is the time to practise what I propose, to let go and leave the development of a new politics to you, the reader. I include, as a resource, a list of further reading, and of journals and websites where many knowledgeable and experienced people are sharing their ideas and would welcome your collaboration. As Jeremy Corbyn put it: 'At the end of the day, human beings want to do things together. We want to do things collectively.'

Notes

Preface

1 Italo Calvino, *Hermit in Paris: Autobiographical Writings*. Translated from the Italian by Martin McLaughlin (selected, with a preface, by Ester Calvino), New York: Pantheon Books, 2003.

1 A New Politics of Knowledge

1 A full discussion of the implications of this for epistemology would draw on the work of Thomas Kuhn, especially his *Structure of Scientific Revolutions*, 2nd edn (Chicago and London: University of Chicago Press, 1970); but that is beyond the scope of this short book.

2 See interview with Aristedes Baltaz, the Co-ordinator of Syriza's programme for government, and later Minister for Education in the Syriza government, by H. Wainwright, www.redpepper.org.uk/greece-syriza-shines-a-light.

3 Tom Hazeldene, 'Revolt of the Rustbelt', *New Left Review*, 105, May/June 2017.

4 F. Hayek, 'The Use of Knowledge in Society' in Hayek, *Individualism and Economic Order*, London, 1949. See also Hayek, *Individualism and Economic Order*, p. 14, for his fullest statement of his individualist understanding of knowledge. For a fuller critique of this understanding, see H. Wainwright, *Arguments for a New Left: Answering the Free Market Right*, Oxford: Blackwell, 1994, pp. 41–65.

5 Michael Polanyi, *The Tacit Dimension*, London: Routledge, 1966, and *Personal Knowledge: Towards a Post-Critical Philosophy*, University of Chicago Press, 1958.

6 The late Marco Aurelio García, a founding member of the PT in São Paulo, Professor at the University of São Paulo (Campinas), and then foreign policy advisor to President Lula.

7 Beatrice Webb, *Our Partnership*, London, New York and Toronto: Longman, 1948, p. 120; also https:// digital.library.lse.ac.uk/collections/webb (typescript diary entry for 29 December 1940).

8 Beatrice Webb, online typescript diary entry for 11 August 1940.

9 John Maynard Keynes, 'Am I a Liberal?' [1925], *The Nation & Athenaeum*, Part I, 8 August 2015, pp. 563–4, and Part II, 15 August 2015, pp. 587–8.

10 A radical minority – mainly of '68ers' – in the NUT campaigned strongly and effectively on issues of gender and race and the curriculum, and won significant victories – for example with the Inner

London Educational Authority in the 1970s and early 1980s.

11 Paulo Freire, *Pedagogy of the Oppressed*, 30th edn, London: Bloomsbury, 2000.

12 For a discussion of the importance of understandings of knowledge in social movements and struggles in the South, see Boaventura de Sousa Santos (ed.), *Another Knowledge is Possible*, London: Verso, 2007.

13 Williams, *The Long Revolution*, with Introduction by Anthony Barnett, Cardigan, Wales: Parthian Books, 2011.

14 In Tredegar, in South Wales, the local miners' lodge used the union as the basis for organizing access to healthcare, not only for miners and their families but for the whole community. They created the Tredegar Working Men's Medical Aid Society. By the 1920s, the society included 95 per cent of the town's population and employed five GPs, a specialist surgeon, two pharmacists, a dentist, a physiotherapist and a domiciliary nurse, from all of whom care would be free at the point of use. There were similar developments elsewhere in South Wales and in the North of England. These were all to influence Bevan's plan for a National Health Service.

15 Ralph Miliband, *Parliamentary Socialism*, London: Allen & Unwin, 1961.

16 Lewis Minkin, *The Contentious Alliance*, Edinburgh University Press, 1992, p. 58.

17 *The Times*, 28 October 1946.

18 In 1941, there was the National Productivity Advisory Council; in 1947, the Economic Planning

Board; and finally, in 1962, the National Economic Development Council – only abolished, by John Major, in 1992.

19 Minkin, *The Contentious Alliance* (1992).
20 E. P. Thompson, 'Outside the Whale', in Thompson, *Out of Apathy*, London: New Left Books, 1960.
21 E. P. Thompson, *The Making of the English Working Class*, London: Penguin Books, 1960, p. 781.
22 See the memoirs of Peggy Duff, an impressive leader of CND: *Left, Left, Left*, London: Allison & Busby, 1971.
23 Alex Nunns, *The Candidate*, London, New York: OR Books, 2016.
24 'What We've Achieved So Far', an interview with Jeremy Corbyn by Leo Panitch and Hilary Wainwright, *Red Pepper*, December 2015: www.redpepper.org.uk.
25 These are the two whose history I have followed. Many of the same points might be made about the Bolivian Movement for Socialism (MAS), and probably others too.

2 The New Politics in Practice

1 Mike Cooley, *Architect or Bee? The Human Price of Technology*, London: Hogarth Press, 1978.
2 The management methdology laid out most systematically by F.W. Taylor in the 1890s and 1900s and developed in practice by institutions as apparently varied as the Ford Motor Company and the Soviet state. 'Taylorism' insists that workers' practical knowledge, exercised intuitively in the course of

their labour, is an insurmountable obstacle to management control – which requires that knowledge of
production is codified and centralized. Taylor argues
not only that practical knowledge of any economic
relevance can be centralized, but that it is vastly more
efficient to do so; he boasted of his system that 'the
workman is told minutely just what he is to do and
how he is to do it; any improvement which he makes
upon the orders given to him is fatal to success'.

3 All unattributed quotes in this section come from the
first meeting of the combine committee that discussed
and agreed upon the idea of the alternative corporate
plan, quoted extensively in ch. 1 of H. Wainwright and
D. Elliot, *The Lucas Plan: A New Trade Unionism in
the Making*, London: Allison & Busby, 1979.

4 Ibid., p. 84.

5 See H. Beynon and H. Wainwright, *The Workers'
Report on Vickers: The Vickers Shop Stewards Combine Committee Report on Work, Wages, Rational-
isation, Closures and Rank-and-File Organisation in a
Multinational Company*. London: Pluto Press, 1979.

6 See Maggie Mort, *Building the Trident Network: A
Study of the Enrollment of People, Knowledge and
Machines*, Cambridge, MA: MIT Press, 2001, for the
full story of BAEC.

7 See Steven Schofield, 'Defence Diversification or
Arms Conversion: Why Labour Needs a Programme
for Nuclear and Conventional Disarmament', 2015,
The Less Network: lessnet.org.uk.

8 This was the idea, pioneered in Latin America
– especially Brazil and Uruguay – of opening up

municipal budgets to rigorously organized popular participation. There is an extensive literature on this experience. See, for example, Boaventura de Sousa Santos, 'Participatory Budgeting in Porto Alegre: Towards a Redistributive Democracy', *Politics & Society*, 26 (4), December 1998, pp. 451–510; Archon Fung and Erik Ohlin Wright (eds.), *Deepening Democracy: Institutional Innovations in Empowered Participatory Governance*, London: Verso, 2003; Daniel Chavez and Benjamin Goldfrank, *The Left in the City: Attempting Participatory Democracy in Latin American Municipalities*, London: Latin American Bureau, 2003; Rebecca Albers, *Inventing Local Democracy: Grassroots Politics in Brazil*, Boulder, CO: Lynne Rienner, 2000; H. Wainwright, *Reclaim the State: Experiments in Popular Democracy*, Calcutta: Seagull Books, 2009, pp. 117–90. See also a caution-ary note on its perverse dynamics: Evelina Dagnino, 'Citizenship: A Perverse Confluence', *Development in Practice*, 17 (4–5), August 2007, pp. 549–56.

9 For a detailed study based on interviews with all of the main actors, including management, unions and communities, see H. Wainwright, *Public Service Reform but Not as we Know It*, London: Compass, 2013.

10 See Mary Kaldor's interesting use of this concept in the context of military technology in *The Baroque Arsenal*, New York: Hill & Wang, 1981.

11 Quoted in Wainwright, *Public Service Reform*.

12 A good history of this movement, including Stewart Brand and the *Whole Earth Catalog*, is provided by

Fred Turner in *From Counterculture to Cyberculture: Stewart Brand, the Whole Earth Network, and the Rise of Digital Utopianism*, University of Chicago Press, 2006.

13 M. Fuster Morell, 'Governance of Online Creation Communities: Provision of Infrastructure for the Building of Digital Commons', dissertation, European University Florence, 2010, p. 5, www.onlinecreation. info/?page_id=338.

14 See Nick Srniceck, *Platform Capitalism*, Cambridge: Polity, 2017, for an excellent analysis of these new forms of organization characteristic of some parts of contemporary capitalism, and see Robin Murray on 'Platform Co-operativism' in 'Post-post-Fordism in the Era of Platforms', *New Formations*, 84/85 (09), 2015.

15 Mayo Fuster Morell, presentation given at the 'Crisis of Politics; the Politics of Crisis' seminar at the Transnational Institute, Cape Town, 2017.

3 From Cells to Transitions

1 Thus, human development is the core of a new politics from the left and of socialism for today. Here, the work of Michael Lebowitz is especially rich, particularly his analyses of Marx's conception of the relation between self-change and change in circumstances, and hence the importance of practical struggle for the full development of human capacities. See Michael Lebowitz, *The Socialist Alternative*, New York: Monthly Review Press, 2010.

2 See Robin Murray, 'Global Civil Society and the Rise of the Civil Economy', in Mary Kaldor, Henrietta L. Moore and Sabine Selchow, eds., *Global Civil Society Yearbook 2012: Ten Years of Reflection*, Basingstoke: Palgrave Macmillan, 2012.

3 See David Harvey, *The Enigma of Capital*, London: Profile Books, 2010.

4 Fairtrade, however, now faces a serious threat from major UK supermarkets, led by Sainsbury's, who are planning to replace the Fairtrade mark with their own Fairly Traded assertion, undermining decades of hard-won rights for hundreds of thousands of co-operative producers.

5 I draw here on the work of social historian and teacher Stephen Yeo, who has assiduously and with great political insight documented the early history of co-operativism: see 'Towards Co-operative Politics: Using Early to Generate Late Socialism', *Journal of Co-operative Studies*, 42 (3), December 2009, pp. 22–35; and of Cilla Ross and the Co-operative College, who have produced a valuable survey on political support for co-operatives across four countries with a significant co-operative sector.

6 Section 137 of the 1972 Local Government Act. This was a very important legal provision that justified most of the GLC's more radical and innovative work. The Conservative government repealed this section as a first step towards restraining its capacities – completed by abolition.

7 For example, Hugh Dalton, Attlee's Chancellor of the Exchequer, is reported as saying to his Private

Secretary: 'We're going to nationalize the Bank. We don't know how, but we're going to do it. Get the appropriate fellow to draw up the plans.'

8 See Mary Mellor, *Debt or Democracy: Public Money for Sustainability and Social Justice,* London: Pluto, 2015. Here she argues that it is the privatization of money – and not money itself – that has fuelled social exploitation and environmental destruction. Money could, by contrast, help us to advance towards an economy based on social justice and sustainability, but only if it is reclaimed for the public. Such public money can facilitate the provision of economic security and sustainable livelihoods for all; but only if there is robust democratic control over monetary decision-making, along with vigorous oversight of its implementation.

9 See Michael Polanyi, *Personal Knowledge: Towards a Post-Critical Philosophy*, University of Chicago Press, 1958.

4 Conclusions: On Questions of Political Strategy and Organization

1 For the full quote, see Raymond Williams, *The Long Revolution*, with Introduction by Anthony Barnett, Cardigan, Wales: Parthian Books, 2011.

2 One of the main points raised by Michael Polanyi, the principal theorist of tacit knowledge, was to highlight its importance in scientific experiments, which are essentially collaborative processes.

3 Blog of Grenfell Action Group, https://grenfell actiongroup.wordpress.com/. This blog, read in total, chronologically, is a telling and vivid indictment of a

housing system in which the needs and concerns of residents are the lowest priority and cutting short-term financial costs is the highest.

4 For an excellent analysis of the policies of austerity that led up to the human-made tragedy of Grenfell, see Vickie Cooper and David Whyte, *The Anatomy of Violence*, London: Pluto Press, 2012.

5 See Oscar Reyes and Bertie Russell, 'Fearless Cities', *Red Pepper*, August/September 2017.

6 Ralph Miliband, *Parliamentary Socialism*, London: Allen & Unwin, 1961.

7 H. Wainwright, *Labour: A Tale of Two Parties*, London: Chatto & Windus, 1987.

8 Richard Crossman, 'Introduction' to Walter Bagehot, *The English Constitution*, London: Fontana, 1963.

9 It should be noted that the right of the party have, under a leader from the left, shown no equivalent respect for the party's norms of unity in the build-up to a general election.

10 The Stop the War coalition was formed in 2001 to mobilize resistance against attack on the Middle East by the USA, UK and others, waged in the name of the 'War on Terror'.

11 Miliband, *Parliamentary Socialism*, pp. 13–14.

12 Reyes and Russell, 'Fearless Cities'.

13 Ibid.

14 I hear from well-informed inside sources that the party's apparatus of full-time regional organizers united against the Corbyn leadership at the 2016 party conference – the first one after his second successful election to the leadership.

Further Reading and Resources

Here I list books, articles and websites that have not been referred to in footnotes but are nevertheless likely to be useful for any reader interested in the arguments in this book. Most of the books are recent, but I have also included some older books to which I always find it useful to return.

Publications

Alternative Models of Public Ownership, Report to the Shadow Chancellor of the Exchequer and Shadow Secretary of State for Business, Energy and Industrial Strategy, Labour Party, 2017.

Arrighi, Giovanni, and Beverly Silver, *Chaos and Governance in the Modern System*, Minneapolis: University of Minnesota Press, 1999.

Barnett, Anthony, *The Lure of Greatness: England's Brexit and America's Trump*, London: Unbound, 2017.

Bauwens, Michel, and Vasilis Kostakis, *Peer to Peer: The Commons Manifesto*, London: Westminster Press, 2018.

Bauwens, Michel, Vasilis Kostakis, Stacco Tronso and Ann Marie Utratel, *Commons Transition and P2P: A Primer*, Amsterdam: Transnational Institute (TNI) and P2P Foundation, 2017; www.tni.org.

Further Reading and Resources

Beynon, Huw, *Working for Ford*, London: Penguin, 1984.

Bhaskar, Roy, *Enlightened Common Sense*, Abingdon: Routledge, 2016.

Boltanski, Luc, and Eve Chiapello, *The New Spirit of Capitalism*, London: Verso, 2005.

Buraway, Michael, *Extended Case Method, Four Decades, Four Great Transformations and One Theoretical Tradition*, Berkeley: University of California Press, 2009.

Cockshott, W. Paul, and Allin Cottrell, *Towards a New Socialism*, Nottingham: Spokesman, 1993.

Crouch, Colin, *The Strange Non-Death of Neo-Liberalism*, Cambridge: Polity, 2011.

Cumbers, Andrew, *Reclaiming Public Ownership*, London: Zed Books, 2012.

De Angelis, Massimo, *Omnia Sunt Communia: On the Commons and the Transformation to Postcapitalism*, London: Zed Books, 2017.

Harvey, David, *Marx, Capital and the Madness of Economic Reason*, London: Profile Books, 2017.

Hess, Charlotte, and Elinor Ostrom (eds.), *Understanding Knowledge as a Commons*, Cambridge, MA: MIT Press, 2011.

Kahler, Miles (ed.), *Networked Politics*, New York: Cornell University Press, 2009.

Kaldor, Mary, and Sabine Selchow (eds.), *Subterranean Politics in Europe*, London: Palgrave Macmillan, 2015.

Karitzis, Andreas, *The European Left in Times of Crisis: The Lessons from Greece*, Amsterdam: Transnational Institute, 2017.

Klein, Naomi, *No is Not Enough*, London: Allen Lane, 2017.

Laskos, Christos, and Euclid Tsakaolotos, *Crucible of Resistance*, London: Pluto, 2015.

Leys, Colin, *Market-Driven Politics*, London: Verso, 2001.

Mair, Peter, *Ruling the Void: The Hollowing of Western Democracy*, London: Verso, 2013.

Further Reading and Resources

Margetts, Helen, Peter John, Scott Hale and Taha Yasseri, *Political Turbulence: How Social Media Shape Collective Action*, Princeton University Press, 2016.

Mason, Paul, *PostCapitalism: A Guide to our Future*, London: Allen Lane, 2015.

Mazzucato, Mariana, *The Entrepreneurial State: Debunking Public vs Private Sector Myths*, London: Anthem, 2013.

McAlevey, Jane, *Raising Expectations (and Raising Hell): My Decade Fighting for the Labour Movement*, London: Verso, 2014.

Mellor, Mary, *The Future of Money: From Financial Crisis to Public Resource*, London: Pluto Press, 2010.

Merrifield, Andy, *The Amateur: The Pleasures of Doing What You Love*. London: Verso, 2017.

Minkin, Lewis, *The Blair Supremacy: A Study in the Politics of Labour's Management*, Manchester University Press, 2014.

Nairn, Tom, and Angelo Quattrochi, *The Beginning of the End: France, May 1968*, London: Verso, 1998.

Outhwaite, William, *Brexit: Sociological Responses*, London and New York: Anthem, 2017.

Panitch, Leo, and Sam Gindin, *The Making of Global Capitalism*, London: Verso, 2012.

Panitch, Leo, and Colin Leys, *The End of Parliamentary Socialism*, London: Verso, 2001.

Rowbotham, Sheila, '1968: Springboard for Women's Liberation', in *New World Coming: The Sixties and the Shaping of Global Consciousness*, ed. Karen Dubinsky, Catherine Krull, Susan Lord et al., Toronto: Between the Lines, 2009.

Santos, Boaventura de Sousa (ed.), *Another Knowledge is Possible*, London: Verso, 2008.

Segal, Lynne, *Radical Happiness: Moments of Collective Joy*, London: Verso, 2017.

Seymour, Richard, *Corbyn: The Strange Rebirth of Radical Politics*, London: Verso, 2016.

Further Reading and Resources

Smucker, Jonathan, *Hegemony How-To: A Road Map for Radicals*, Oakland: AK Press, 2017.

Srnicek, Nick, and Alex Williams, *Inventing the Future: Postcapitalism and a World without Work*, London: Verso, 2016.

Standing, Guy, *A Precariat Charter: From Denizens to Citizens*, London: Bloomsbury, 2014.

Websites and Organizations

Beyond the Technological Revolution,
www.beyondthetechrevolution.com.
Beyond the Technological Revolution is a four-year research project led by Carlota Perez, as a continuation of the work done for her 2002 book *Technological Revolutions and Financial Capital: The Dynamics of Bubbles and Golden Ages* (Cheltenham: Edward Elgar). Also see carlotaperez.org.

Centre for Local Economic Strategy (CLES),
www.cles.org.
The aim of CLES is 'to achieve social justice, good local economies and effective public services for everyone, everywhere'.

Compass, www.compassonline.org.uk
Compass provides a generous spirited forum for sharing and debating ideas and for collaborating on transformative action between progressive activists across political parties and amongst social movements.

Momentum, www.peoplesmomentum.com.
Momentum is a grassroots campaigning network of over 23,000 members and 150 local groups, which evolved out of Jeremy Corbyn's 2015 leadership election campaign.

Further Reading and Resources

Networked Politics was a series of seminars and publications intended as a contribution to the continuing debates and practical experiments concerning new forms of political organization in an age of movements and networks

Its interesting material is archived at https://www.tni.org/en/search?search=Networked+Politics.

New Economics Foundation (NEF), http://neweconomics.org, and New Economy Organisers Network (NEON), www.new-economyorganisers.org.

The New Economics Foundation defines itself as a people-driven think tank committed to meeting the urgent need for a new economy, and is associated with a network of new economy organizers, with over 1,600 UK organizers from 900 different civil society groups. NEON runs training and support campaigns to help progressives win social, economic and environmental justice. Both NEF and NEON are committed to building a new economy where people really take control, through taking action now.

Novara, www.novaramedia.com.

Novara Media is an independent media organization, addressing the issues – from a crisis of capitalism to racism and climate change – that are set to define the twenty-first century.

P2P Foundation, www.p2pfoundation.net.

This foundation is a global network of researchers, activists and citizens monitoring and promoting actions geared towards a transition to a Commons-based society.

Public Services International Research Unit,
www.psiru.org.

PSIRU researches the privatization and restructuring of public services around the world, and the alternatives, with special focus on water, energy, waste management and healthcare. It has documented the failures of privatization.

Further Reading and Resources

Radical housing network,
www.radicalhousingnetwork.org
An association of groups fighting for housing justice.

Red Pepper is a bi-monthly magazine and website of left politics and culture. Readers may be especially interested in issue 212 (February/March 2017), 'Resistance is Fertile', on social movement knowledge.

The World Transformed (TWT),
www.theworldtransformed.org.
TWT is a celebration of politics, art, music, culture and community.

Transnational Institute (TNI), www.tni.org.
The Transnational Institute strengthens international social movements with rigorous research, reliable information, sound analysis and constructive proposals that advance progressive, democratic policy change and common solutions to global problems.

We Own It, www.weownit.org.uk.
We Own It campaigns for public services run for people, not profit.